*Kamera is published
5 times per year by*
Oldcastle Books Ltd
P O Box 394
Harpenden
AL5 1XJ

www.kamera.co.uk

Next issue available October 2003

Distribution:
Turnaround,
3 Olympia Trading Estate,
Coburg Rd, London, N22 6TZ

Printing
Cox & Wyman

Editor
John Atkinson

KAMERA
The Old Surgery
9 Pulford Road
Leighton Buzzard
LU7 1AB

Tel: 01525 373896
Email: editor@kamera.co.uk

Typesetting and design
Paul Brazier

Advertising:
ads@kamera.co.uk

01582 761264

Subscriptions
5 issues
£25 inc P&P for UK
£40 inc P&P outside UK
see page 96 for special offer

Legal
Kamera is copyright © 2003
Oldcastle Books Ltd
ISBN 1-904048-97-8

All rights reserved. No part of this book may be reproduced, stored in or introduced into a retrieval system, or transmitted, in any form or by any means (electronic, mechanical, photocopying, recording or otherwise) without the written commission of the publisher.

2003

"GOOD WRITING ON FILM"

– it doesn't sound that hard, does it? You would like to think that every film magazine would aspire to such a modest ambition. But think about it. When was the last time you bought a publication dedicated to the movies that wasn't just a vehicle for consumer advertising disguised as a breathless glorification of the latest over-hyped Hollywood product? I know you know what I'm talking about – those mags where the copywriting on the ads is more thoughtful than in the reviews (*** out of ***** it is, then). Since its inception three years ago, www.kamera.co.uk has tried hard to raise the expectations of film fans when it comes to reading about their favourite past-time. Unlike virtually ever other film web site that springs to mind, kamera.co.uk is not hung up on the latest blockbusters. That's not to say that we're down on Hollywood – we just don't think they need our help when there's so much else going on in world cinema that's worth writing about (although we're happy to give credit where it's due – last year one of the out-and-out raves we gave was to *Spider-Man*...). So while kamera.co.uk usually gets round to covering the latest box office monarch, it's those other, smaller films we find most interesting – US indies, foreign language films, dare we say it ... art house flicks. Which brings us to this 1st edition of the *Kamera* magazine. The same points stand. Here's what passes for a mission statement in these here parts:

- *Kamera* is interested in what's going on in the whole world of film, now and in the past.
- We do think much American cinema is great, but there's more to life.
- Opening weekend grosses are fun, but so what?
- There are film-makers who are happy to talk more widely than just plugging their latest work.
- Documentary and short film deserve your attention.
- There are film-festivals taking place every week somewhere in the world – not just annually in the South of France.
- Just because they are shiny and have lots of extras, not every DVD release is worth getting excited about.
- In the main, books are good things, not something film fans (or magazines) should be embarrassed about enjoying.

We think the content of issue 1 reflects this, and then some. Write and tell us what you think. Oh, and if you don't already, visit the web site. The contents of this issue will eventually appear as part of the 'subscriber' section, but there are new reviews and features posted every week which you won't find in the paper magazine. Spread the word, and come back real soon.

John Atkinson, Editor, KAMERA
editor@kamera.co.uk

What's So Good About 70s American Cinema?

Apparently, it's official. The American cinema of the 1970s was the last Golden Age of movies. Book-ended by *Easy Rider* (1969) and *Heaven's Gate* (1980) – with a significant change of gear thanks to *Star Wars* (1977) – the decade saw the flowering of the Movie Brat generation, inmates who aspired to take over the asylum. Those who did so most vociferously had crashed and burned with varying degrees of injury before the decade's end; those who talked the language of the studios who hired them ended up some of the richest and most powerful men in movies, ever.

These 'facts' are documented in a spate of recent books and films, yet, already, these documents have started to reheat the same themes – the know-it-all Bogdanovich who became lost in his own fantasy; the inextricable links between Scorsese's artistry and his self-destructiveness; the pernicious influence of *Star Wars'* success, etc. Is there a danger that, less than thirty years on, we're already printing the legend?

The tenet is simple enough: if you put The Beatles or Elvis on your front cover, you're gonna sell double. The movie magazine equivalents of the newsagent's shelf hotcake icons are *Star Wars* (1977) and *The Godfather* (1972). Whether this popularity of two films old enough to have mortgages and hairy backs is due to nostalgia or artistry is open to many debates. It is such discussions on Seventies US cinema that

On the following pages, Bob Carroll takes a second look at some of the supposed classics of the period, Ian Haydn Smith wonders if the 70s model Bond is the original Brother, and a host of other *KAMERA* contributors offer up some thoughts on their own favourites – in some cases much-neglected – of the era.

dominate film writing today. The millennial hangover of constant "Best of" listing, the annual release of even newer and improved DVD special editions of modern classics and the new film-makers on the block's reverence to the decade they grew up in have placed the Seventies as the contemporary epicentre of classic cinema. Peter Biskind's wildly successful *Easy Riders, Raging Bulls* was a response to the initial glut of retrospectives on the various Movie Brats by peppering the critical analysis with a history of back lot gossip and box office grosses. What should have been a fun footnote inadvertently wiped the slate, as Biskind's volume inspired even more column inches on that period's cinema. The best of this new bunch is Ryan Gibley's *It Don't Worry Me* which, like Biskind's work, canonises Scorsese, Lucas, Coppola, Altman and Spielberg, with the likes of Demme, Schrader, Friedkin, Polanski, Bogdanovich, DePalma and Ashby populating the second tier.

This anointing of the Seventies as the new Golden Age is good for film studies students, a breed derided for their ignorance of cinema prior to BC (Before Chewbacca), as it opens up an accessible and available body of work for them to explore. With many of these chosen directors still working today and even more younger film-makers obsessively following their lead, it acts as a way of legitimising recent movies, whose direct relation to the accepted classics of the Seventies places them ahead of more transgressive or experimental works. Yet

despite the benefits of this lionization, it does worry me!

Before you dress me in a jester costume and call me a fool, I'll profess my respect for all of the above directors and agree that their achievements in the Seventies are enviable. But there is more to Seventies cinema than the bearded, white, middle-class male wunderkinds who had been given the keys to the kingdom and this disproportionate focus on them is damaging. Naming the works of the above dozen directors as the cream of their shared decade's crop should be a starting point for a broader study, not the be-all and end-all it is becoming.

In the US alone many older directors also took advantage of the crumbling of a studio system that had reined them in during their careers until then. For me Sam Peckinpah's best work is not the butchered and restored *The Wild Bunch* (1969) but his streamlined genre shakers like *The Getaway* (1972) and *Cross of Iron* (1977). Don Siegel turned out the impressive, unhindered run of *The Beguiled*, *Dirty Harry* (both 1971) and *Charley Varrick* (1973). Sidney Lumet's prolific productivity means that despite the praise his cynical sweatfests *Dog Day Afternoon* (1975) and *Network* (1976) receive, he never seems directly credited for their merits. *Deliverance* (1972), *Papillon* (1973), *Marathon Man* (1976) and let us not forget Kubrick's continued brilliance during those ten years, are all testaments to the currently ignored remainder of US cinema from that era. These films are as important as the

Chinatowns (1974) and *French Connections* (1971) to the maturity of current movies, so it must be the white hair and previously existing work of their directors that is at odds with the Young Turk criteria that make the coked up kids such good copy. Of course, Altman really fits in better with the less reputed pensioner list but he has continued to produce celebrated cinema, albeit intermittently, and is almost certainly P T Anderson's biggest influence despite fresh protests by the *Magnolia* (1999) director.

Moving across the Atlantic and Pacific now, it is surprising how many celebrated world auteurs seemed to clear a path in the Seventies. Akira Kurosawa and Sergio Leone carried on working yet nothing they produced matched their masterpieces of the Sixties and Eighties. The French New Wave vandals seemed to have lost their quality control during those ten years, the only film that stands the test of time being Truffaut's *Day for Night* (1972). Maybe as a response to the bold, Europeanised spectacles that Hollywood was producing world cinema seemed to internalise. The works of Tarkovsky, Fassbinder, Bergman, Herzog and others marked a retreat into more obscure, less populist themes and styles. Hollywood imports had embraced the lessons of the New Wave and welded them into their popular genres. The attitude appeared to be; if the Yanks were importing what the Europeans once excelled at then the Europeans needed to take things a couple of steps further to see if the Yanks would follow.

The reverse happened over the other side of the globe, where in a response to the more complex product America was sending to them, India, Australia and Hong Kong fell back on their own blockbuster genres to entertain the locals. This homegrown industry boom unintentionally sowed the financial seeds for the next generation of auteurs to flourish.

Britain, whose production was essentially funded by Hollywood, initially produced some fantastic cinema; *Get Carter* (1971), *Don't Look Now* (1973) and *The Wicker Man* (1973). These pushed boundaries by mixing pulp source material with humanist values to produce some fractured masterpieces that still puzzle and inspire today. Even if the studio had no idea what the likes of Ashby and Coppola were doing they could appreciate the eventual success, but British directors like Nic Roeg and Mike Hodges were less fortunate and their money to make unconventional works dried up over the second half of the Seventies.

One cannot help but wonder what classics are gathering dust due to the laziness of us film critics regurgitating articles on *The Exorcist* (1973)? What foreign opuses never received distribution in the US or UK due to the two year runs of *Jaws* (1975) on many screens? Have the pretensions of dated yet still revered films like *Taxi Driver* (1976) forced many a decent journeyman to ruin a good script by overreaching for meaning and significance in it? There is an unseen legacy to the creative freedom granted to that batch of directors. It halted a cinematic dialogue about the decade. Very few of the films (Demme, Ashby and Altman works excepted) were concerned with current problems. What were *American Graffiti* (1973), *Chinatown* or *New York, New York* (1977) but nostalgic paeans to rotten genres? Bogdanovich's *What's Up, Doc?* (1972) was sold to the public as "A screwball comedy. Remember them?" You'd be hard pressed to find any cinema dealing with the oil crisis, the repeated attempts to assassinate President Ford or the murders at the Munich Olympics from this period. Much of the Movie Brats output had little to say about their times, as their only touchstones with reality was the cinema they had immersed themselves into. Even Coppola's Vietnam epic *Apocalypse Now* (1979) had more in common with Joseph Conrad's Victorian-era *Heart of Darkness* than the real experiences of the youth sent to that hell.

And then we arrive at *Star Wars*. Not being one of its detractors, I can nonetheless recognise the creative blight it unleashed onto the Eighties. When the last old school studio heads popped their collective clogs by the dawn of the Seventies the big conglomerates moved in and bought themselves a studio each. Executives were promoted from the tinned goods and toiletries divisions and put in charge of a creative, if mass-produced, medium. They had no idea. The likes of Ashby got away with giving them the old lady/wacky kid suicidal sex comedy *Harold and Maude* (1971) and as long as Joe Public bought tickets and popcorn the suits at Paramount could breath a sigh of relief. Once the cookie cutter morality and merchandising possibilities of Darth Vadar and Luke Skywalker were dropped into their lap, they had a model for the kind of consumer goods they wanted to develop and to hell with vigilante cabbies or freewheeling Phillip Marlowe comedies with bad sound. Like the independent blockade runner in *Star Wars'* opening shot, the rebellious nature of Seventies film-making was captured and destroyed by the enormous and rapidly advancing Star Destroyer of corporate business.

Still, it is churlish to deny the new level of quality and intelligence that Scorsese, Coppola and many of the others brought to our ABC's over those ten years. One can't help but feel a rush knowing that a thirteen year old sitting down to a DVD of *The Godfather* is about to take an incredible cinematic adventure. Maybe this future Tarantino or pubescent Fincher will switch off halfway through finding the Mafia values, classical editing and focus on relationships as foreign and outdated as the world presented in *Russian Ark* (2002). But probably he'll start with "I believe in America" move onto "I love the smell of napalm in the morning" and end up with "He'd kill us if he got the chance" and realise making cinema of technical scope, human detail and mind expanding entertainment is their calling.

Bob Carroll

Voodoo Chic –
Live and Let Die
and the
influence of
Blaxploitation

Barry Adamson's '007: A Phantasy Bond Theme' offers a pastiche of the classic James Bond narrative. In it, the hero is a small Jamaican boy whose dream is to be the world's greatest spy. Following another successful mission, he finally wins an audience with the Queen, who proclaims him the defender of the realm, announcing that 'If we're ever in trouble or under attack, have no fear for Bond is black!' Certainly one of the lighter tracks on Adamson's brooding, anti-racist album, Soul Murder, the song is also one of its cleverest. In addition to using a familiar icon from which to question mass entertainment's culpability in reinforcing outdated values – in this case British

Imperialism – the song highlights the very nature of the Bond films, which have never shied from the appropriation and reinterpretation of other cultures. Nowhere is this more apparent than in the 1973 instalment, *Live and Let Die*.

Following the exhaustion of cold war narratives – at least until the1980s, when East/West politics was heating up as the nuclear arms race again headed towards critical point – the departure of Sean

Connery, and the decline in the Bond franchise's popularity, Harry Saltzman and Albert Broccoli found themselves adrift, directionless in their pursuit of another box office hit. Their solution was daring and more successful than they could possibly have imagined. They chose to film Ian Fleming's second and most problematic novel, *Live and Let Die*. The story of a black SMERSH agent shipping gold doubloons into the US, the novel was always considered unfilmable because of its racist rhetoric, a throwback to the period in which the novel was written and, more specifically, the privileged background of Fleming himself. What made the film possible was the emergence of a genre that would give a new spin on Fleming's story.

In the early 1970s, a number of independent films proved that there was a large black audience that had so far been unrepresented by mainstream American cinema. Melvin Van Peebles' *Sweet Sweetback's Baadass Song* (1971), a film 'Dedicated to all the Brothers and Sisters who have had enough of the Man,' was an independent production that showed the studios how much money they were missing out on in not catering for a larger proportion of the American Diaspora. The result was a series of films, rapidly decreasing in quality and originality, which attempted to redress the balance. Beginning with Gordon Park's *Shaft* (1971), Blaxploitation films offered up a mix of sex and violence in which the put-upon black man (and eventually woman, in the form of Pan Grier and Tamara

Dobson) would rebel against his white aggressor, or the 'brother' who was under the command of 'the Man'. Yet, for all their surface radicalism, these later films were the product of the system that produced them, merely nudging the injustice that existed in the urban squalor of the real ghettos, and a world away from the anger of Van Peebles' film.

This dichotomy of danger within a safe environ – these films never went so far as to completely destroy the status quo – was the perfect platform for screenwriter Tom Mankiewicz, who had written *Diamonds are Forever* (1971) and would pen the next film in the series, *The Man with the Golden Gun* (1974), which was to kung-fu movies what *Live and Let Die* was to Blaxploitation. In his screenplay, the battle between East and West, as well as the very notion of world domination, was disposed of, in favour of something more in keeping with the times. The gold smuggling of the novel was replaced by heroin trafficking, and in the place of a black, Oxbridge educated, Soviet trained psychopath, was a voodoo obsessed West Indian, who also disguised himself as the godfather of Harlem's crime world. Articulate wordplay and high-tech terminology was replaced by street talk and cultural myths. And the new Bond didn't just have to battle for his life, he was fighting the forces that wanted to control his afterlife too.

Mankiewicz took the template of the Blaxploitation genre and inverted it. The race of the hero and 'The Man' were reversed. Street talk was no longer a symbol of emancipation, being instead a threatening presence. And white, red and blue were the colours of good against black, green and gold. Added to the mix was the 'taboo' of a mixed relationship between a black man and a white woman (*Sweetback* could not resist this cliché, but at least managed a degree of subversion – the woman was hardly coerced into the relationship).

With few exceptions, Blaxploitation films confined their action to urban settings. *Live and Let Die*, like all Bond films, takes place in more than one country (a fact encapsulated in its McCartney-penned theme song, which crosses rock, pop and reggae). The link between Harlem and the outside world was fear. If the urban myth of the brutal Mr Big plagued the streets of Harlem, Dr Kananga and his exploitation of voodoo's spiritual power extended his grasp to the Deep South and the Carribbean. That Big and Kananga were the same person elevated the black crime lord to the role of mythic villain whilst simultaneously reducing the diplomat to being nothing more than a drug peddling criminal.

The enduring popularity of this film, over many other Bond films that preceded and followed it, suggests that it is more than a facsimile or rip off of a genre whose films have mostly been forgotten. For as much as it copies elements of the Blaxploitation genre, it also fed into it. Many of the Blaxploitation films were equally guilty of stealing from the Bond formula of sex, spies, guns and action. Both Fred Williamson and Richard Roundtree were as much influenced by the Bond persona as they were by characters from earlier crime dramas. And if you thought Halle Berry's Jinx was the first attempt at a credible female counterpart to Bond (in *Die Another Day*, 2002), watch Tamara Dobson in *Cleopatra Jones* (1973).

Live and Let Die is problematic in its representation of race. And yet it is exactly for that reason that it remains one of the most fascinating of the Bond films. Unlike the recent spate of films starring Pierce Brosnan, it belongs to an era which attempted to tackle the issues around it, no matter how misguided those intentions were. (Don't be fooled by the recent events in Korea and their appearance in *Die Another Day*. At best, the timing is coincidental.) Less a white man's Blaxploitation film than an entertainment that fed into that genre as much as it took from it, it now stands as an essential work of that era.

Ian Haydn Smith

Breezy
(Clint Eastwood, 1973)

She is Breezy - Edith Alice Breezerman (Kay Lenz) - a 'hippie chick', one could say, passing the time in early seventies Los Angeles. She fixes on 'older man' Frank Harmon (William Holden) - and the film's big question, asked without a trace of rhetoric, is whether this relationship can work. She insists that she's a good force to be around, and so she proves to be: she gets Frank thinking about his life, his age, and whether it would be impolite to take up this opportunity. He cares for her -

she's so innocent, and yet perceptive, that it hurts; and yet when he says 'I just cannot cope with it,' he's trying to choose between comfortable solitude and being with a woman but worrying whether he can love her enough.

Breezy has been rather inexplicably neglected, seeing that it is one of a series of late sixties and early seventies films lucky to have been blessed with late-period William Holden, not to mention the fact that it is a film directed by Clint Eastwood when he was undoubtedly the biggest star in the world. By 1973 Eastwood had already helmed two films, the decent thriller *Play Misty For Me* (1971) and the delicious, serene western *High Plains Drifter* (1972), to add to the superstardom that came with his performance as *Dirty Harry* (1971). And so *Breezy* is a sideways step, a intimate story and an opportunity to hone his skill with actors. If it caught audiences, and Universal, off-guard at the time, that reaction has proven hard to shake to this day. Breezy is almost non-existent on VHS or television - it's yet another film for which DVD will be not just a preserver but a saviour.

Coming after *The Wild Bunch* (1969) and before his superb turn in *Network* (1976), Holden's starring role in *Breezy* is a great example of the power of casting. For Holden possessed, in that lined, reasonable face, the good things that explain the young drifter's attraction to his character. And if Kay Lenz displays a contextually accurate lack of self-consciousness about revealing her body, the film also shows Holden bare-chested a number of times, notably in a steam room scene at the gym, where he sits while his friend Bob (Roger C. Carmel) laments his own mid-life situation. Bob looks bloodless and out of shape, while Frank is fit and handsome - it's a scene which very subtly says so much about middle-aged men's views of themselves, and it chimes with Frank's later line to Breezy, 'Nobody matures - they just grow tired.'

Breezy has aged quite well. Eastwood's directing does betray some of the more sappy traits of seventies American film-making - too much long lens, watery music - but even these, in retrospect, are deployed sensitively: the camera is mostly poised and well-placed, and Michel Legrand's score is flattered by being used sparingly. In fact, the moments of near-silence speak volumes in Breezy, and the two leads fill them impressively.

Eastwood has brought romance to the fore only twice in his long career, with *Breezy* and *The Bridges of Madison County* (1995), although *The Gauntlet* (1977) delivers, amid the very entertaining mayhem, some lovely sustained star chemistry between Eastwood and Sondra Locke - arguably their best work together. And *In the Line of Fire* (1993) has Eastwood and Rene Russo getting close under Wolfgang Petersen's direction. *Breezy* is not as moving as *The Bridges...* but it is not as sentimental either, and it contains some choice moments, such as when Frank, thinking himself alone, sits on his bed in the near-darkness, and Breezy's hand curls round his torso to bring him down to her.

Edward Lamberti

Barry Lyndon
(Stanley Kubrick,
1975)

The year is 1975, and Stanley Kubrick's latest film *Barry Lyndon* has just come out. His previous film, *A Clockwork Orange* (1971), tapped into the *Easy Rider* wave of youth-centred film-making, and brought violent teenage rebellion to the political fore. *Barry Lyndon*, however, is his biggest budget film to date and is set to be a flop. Critics are united in their derision: The Los Angeles Times likens it to 'one of those very large... very dull books that exist solely to be seen on coffee tables'. Kubrick's and Warner Bros. gamble was to make a period drama in an era of American film-making obsessed with

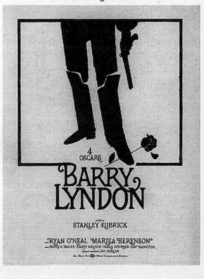

Baxter describes, 'moved to the more stately rhythm of another age – one in which animal appetites and urges flexed their muscles against the constrictions of an ordered society.' His aim was to force the audience to revert their mindset back two hundred years. He had done the opposite with 2001, taking the audience into future time in a way never done before. Whereas 2001's slowness found a place in 1960s psychedelia, in 1975 it was out of place. The rigid beauty of the characters gestures, camera movements and framing, evoked the works of eighteenth century artists Gainsborough and Constable. Ryan O'Neil's Barry is the quintessential tiger-trapped-in-a-cage: when he lashes out at Lord Bullingdon in front of assembled aristocracy, the release of kinetic energy bursts through the screen. Yet O'Neil's performance was grossly misunderstood as wooden, and was overshadowed by exuberant contemporary characters such as De Niro's Johnny Boy in *Mean Streets* (1973). The MTV generation were being born.

Barry Lyndon was a victim of its time, and would be Kubrick's last film of the 1970s. Cinematic art was both acceptable and popular but only, it seemed, for films dealing with the contemporary and immediate. The New Wave of Kubrick devotees such as Scorsese and Coppola would briefly take his crown. Critical re-evaluation however, must firmly place the crown back on the Grand Master's head.

contemporary stories (the two big films of 1975 are *Jaws* and *One Flew Over the Cuckoo's Nest*); how had their gamble gone so wrong?

Kubrick's pet project was a biopic of Napoleon to star the then-emerging Jack Nicholson, and after *2001: A Space Odyssey* (1968) it was tentatively announced by MGM (his studio at the time) as his next film. However, in 1969 Kubrick's biggest supporter on the MGM board was sacked. He was also usurped by a sudden rash of Napoleonic films, including *Waterloo* (1970), and *Eagle in a Cage* (1971). Under these circumstances his project became impossible and he indefinitely postponed Napoleon, but after *A Clockwork Orange*, Kubrick was on a new high. Made for a mere $2m, it had grossed $15.4m worldwide. Kubrick knew that Napoleon was still out of the question, but funding for a different historical epic was now possible.

Kubrick recognised in William Makepeace Thackery's novel *Barry Lyndon* a theme discernable in all his films: man's self-destructive nature. Alongside its universal and contemporary relevance, it was the eighteenth century feel that was fundamental for Kubrick. The film, as John

Tim Smedley

Season of the Witch
A.K.A. Jack's Wife
(George A. Romero, 1973)

Season of the Witch is an early George A. Romero film that fits into the director's reflective phase when he explored some of the most traditional horror conventions (witchcraft, vampires, plague) in an unconventional way. This film attempts to present a modern, feminist take on the witch film, tapping into a middle-aged housewife's paranoia and anxiety about getting old. Although the title is *Jack's Wife*, the husband is mostly absent and distant, and the real story is dominated by the uneasy frisson between Joan Mitchell (Jan White) and her teenage daughter, Nikki (Joedda McClain).

Just as the theme of incest was touched on in *Night of the Living Dead* (1968) where a cannibalistic daughter devours her parents, Joan feels sexually threatened by her daughter. Nikki's blossoming sexuality turns Joan's world upside down. It also causes rows between her and her husband, the latter holds her responsible for ensuring her daughter maintains her virginity. However, Nikki's free and easy attitude towards sex, relationships (and cleaning her teeth!) contrasts with her own submissive and degraded role, which is presented masterfully in the film's opening 'dream sequence'. A typical breakfast scene is transplanted into high expressionist symbolism, we see Joan following her husband through a wood as he eats his breakfast, dispassionately allowing branches to flick back into her face. Jack (Bill Thunhurst) eats eggs (symbolic of new life) and we see a shot of a baby in the grass, reminding us of how everything is inextricably linked back to the sexual drive of nature. Joan sees herself as a young girl in a white dress sitting on a swing, but her husband walks on by without noticing her. He hits her and puts her on a leash and into a cage, a hard hitting series of images that have to sustain us for the rest of the film. After an arresting start, the rest of the film is far too talky with overlong discussions about dope, affairs and morality, and little of the cinematic verve that we have come to expect from Romero. (It is a low budget film, shot for just $100,000 but is completely different to the tense brilliance of *Night of the Living Dead*.)

Romero plays only partially successfully with the age-old fear of witchcraft, which he shows has succumbed, like everything else, to commercial interests. When Joan encounters a practising witch who reads her friend's Tarot cards, she finds out that now anyone can buy spell books and witch

equipment easily, and Joan gets sucked in to this 'alternative world'. As Joan feels more confident and the relationship with her daughter becomes more strained, we are repeatedly reminded that Joan (in contrast to some of her friends) is still attractive. Her daughter tells her, 'You know you really have a great body – you don't normally think of your Mom as having a great body'. Joan wakes up from her repressed life only to masturbate to the sounds of her daughter having sex in the room next door to her, and to later steal her daughter's lover and drive Nikki away. Although Joan believes that her new hobby of spell-casting is changing her luck, Romero doesn't emphasise this as convincingly as he does the vampire theme in *Martin* (1978), and the audience is always aware that the real horror here is the fear of 'ending up a clapped-out old lady'. Sadly, this emphasis works to undermine the film's feminist concerns – perhaps it is not without significance that Romero was getting divorced from his first wife during the film's creation. Not, under any circumstances, to be confused with *Halloween III: Season of the Witch* (1982).

Marcelle Perks

WHAT'S SO GOOD ABOUT 70s AMERICAN CINEMA

A Safe Place
(Henry Jaglom, 1971)

It would be fairly safe to describe Henry Jaglom as something of a one-off. The London-born film-maker has come to be known for two main reasons: 80s flicks including *National Lampoon Goes to the Movies* (1981) and *Can She Bake a Cherry Pie?* (1983), and his apparent omnipresence at film festivals around the globe. Without a doubt more famous than any single one of his films, Jaglom stands as a curious individual and a sporadically interesting film-maker.

A Safe Place was Jaglom's first stab at directing, and is a film that positively brims with his now-trademark weirdness. It stars Tuesday Weld as fragile New Yorker Susan, a woman who apparently can't/won't deal with city life. Handy then, that she seems to possess the ability to cross over into another dimension, where life seems that bit more interesting. This alternate time/place is headed by a man known simply as The Magician (Welles). Susan is sometimes known as Noah. There's also Susan/Noah's unremarkable boyfriend Fred (Proctor), and ex-boyfriend Mitch (Nicholson) – although it's inferred that Mitch might actually be her brother.

A Safe Place hasn't exactly been over-discussed through the years, but I have seen Jean-Luc Godard's name mentioned

in one or two tidbits written about the movie. Comparisons with Godard seem a little off the mark, and if *A Safe Place* recalls the work of any other director, it's probably Godard's compatriot Jean Cocteau, whose playful final work *Le Testament d'Orphée* (1959) offered up a similar tale of time travel and parallel worlds. Cocteau's film, it has to be said, is far more enjoyable, but both pictures share a couple of things in common, such as an air of genuine mischief and some very creaky sets.

Jaglom worked on *Easy Rider*, and was fairly tight with stars Jack Nicholson, Dennis Hopper and Karen Black. After the runaway success of that film, Jaglom reunited with Nicholson for *A Safe Place*, giving the actor a sizeable supporting role. He'd go on to direct Hopper in *Tracks* (1976, one of Jaglom's better-known films), and hooked up with Black for *Can She Bake a Cherry Pie?*

What makes *A Safe Place*'s obscurity fairly surprising is not just that it features Nicholson, but that it was directed by someone who was very much part of the whole *Easy Rider* phenomenon and who also went on to have a recurring association with the films main players; in what proved to be a remarkably busy period for all concerned, Jaglom also turned out in front of the camera for Nicholson's *Drive, He Said* (1971) and Hopper's *The Last Movie* (1971). *A Safe Place* is a title that seems to have genuinely slipped under the radar - all the more remarkable when you think of all the analysis afforded to Hopper's biker flick in the thirty-odd years since it was first released. Perhaps DVD will open up a new audience for this little-seen curio, a milker of the Nicholson cash cow inevitably propelling Jack's leering visage to the forefront of the sleeve...

Darren Arnold

WHAT'S SO GOOD ABOUT 70s AMERICAN CINEMA?

**Piranha
(Joe Dante,
1978),** etc.
'Get out of the water,' bellows Chief Brody (Roy Scheider) as a cloud of crimson in the ocean signals the demise of another hapless swimmer in Steven Spielberg's *Jaws*. Wise words indeed, and not just because of the killer great white shark patrolling the waters around the fictional US seaside town of Amity. The sea is a nasty place, full of all sorts of creatures just waiting for the opportunity to turn you into a fish's supper. Or so a spate of 1970s films would have you believe.

It all started with *Jaws*, which upon its

release in 1975 became the highest-grossing film ever made and dragged the summer season up from a wasteground for B-movies and exploitation flicks into the most commercial time of year. Ironically, though, Jaws inspired a bunch of cheap B-movies which, ahem, rode on the wave of its success.

Of course, *Jaws* couldn't have been more inaccurate about the habits of the great white shark itself. When Peter Benchley wrote the source novel, little was known about them in the public domain and it was easy to turn a mysterious and formidable killing machine into a giant man-eater. In reality, West USA has seen only six human fatalities resulting from great white attacks since 1872 – yet five people (and a dog) are eaten over the course of one weekend in the film.

Hollywood has never been one to let the truth get in the way of a good story and the Jaws spin-offs were no exception. *Piranha* (1978) sees a school of killer fish escape into a holiday resort and consume the residents. A blatant attempt to capitalise on the success of *Jaws*, the film-makers weren't content to let this be any normal swarm of snappers. Instead, they are a secret government weapon, specially bred to feed on humans – hence more gore and a higher body count. Similarly, *Alligator* (1980), in which a gator is flushed down a toilet, and – no doubt thriving on a diet of turds and rats – grows to gigantic proportions and terrorises the sewers of Chicago.

These tongue-in-cheek exploitations of a theme are witty and entertaining. Less so is *The Deep* (1977). Though this focuses on a shipwreck full of morphine and drug-dealer's subsequent scams to get hold of it, the film was another Peter '*Jaws*' Benchley adaptation and preys on people's fear of the sea that the shark flick provoked. This time the monster is a giant moray eel that makes a brief appearance to do some conveniently-timed bad guy biting.

And then it was a case of send in the clones. Excepting the *Jaws* sequels, in which the shark goes from being simply hungry to downright vindictive, there was the farcical Richard Harris vehicle, *Orca* (1977), featuring a vengeful killer whale, and *Up From the Depths* (1979), in which a 'shark-like creature' (even less convincing than *Jaws*'s 'Bruce' rubber shark) lays waste to the inhabitants of a remote Hawaiian island.

The number of recorded shark attacks has actually risen every decade since 1900, *except* in the 1970s. This might just be a coincidence, but you have to wonder whether this was because more people were genuinely scared away from the water. One positive aspect of these movies was that, despite their exaggerated nature, they made people more wary about entering the sea armed with nothing but suntan lotion and an inflatable raft – it is still the world's undiscovered wilderness and holds many hidden dangers. It might not be full of genetically altered piranhas or gluttonous giant sharks, but, as Benchley put it: 'More than 80 per cent of all living things live in the sea. And they all, naturally, have to eat.'

Paul Clarke

Days of Heaven
(Terrence Malick, 1978)

While Spielberg, Scorsese, Kubrick, Coppola and Lucas were busy altering the course of film-making, defining a now infamous 'golden' age of contemporary American cinema, Terrence Malick was slowly fashioning one of the most intriguing and enduring films to come out 1970s Hollywood, *Days of Heaven*. Set in 1916 in the Texas panhandle, the story is beguilingly simple. A couple, Bill and Abby, masquerade as man and wife and travel from the city to the country to work in the wheatfields, with Bill's young sister Linda in tow. The wealthy landowner, who they believe is dying, takes a fancy to Abby. Urged by the opportunistic Bill, she accepts the farmer's offer of marriage and possibly even falls in love. As the farmer shows no signs of dying, jealousies are aroused and suspicions simmer. During a locust

infestation, which destroys the crops, the farmer discovers he has been deceived and attempts to kill Bill, but is killed himself. The three flee and are tracked by a posse who eventually catch up with them and shoot Bill.

On paper, the narrative is as crisp and taut as that of any thriller; edgy, nail-biting, psychologically intense. But on the screen, its elliptical meanderings, long shots detailing the minutiae of nature and the day-to-dayness of working the land, belie its lean 95 minutes, combining to make the film feel more languorous. Malick creates a world unlike any other, painting on a broad visual canvass of seasonal change, where time plays by its own rules and according to its own laws.

So, what kind of film is this? As much (if not more) about land and nature as the characters that inhabit the landscape, stylistically it exhibits a more pronounced identification with European art movies such as *L'Avventura* (1960) than the gritty

realism of *Five Easy Pieces* and *Taxi Driver* or the cynicism of *Network* and *Apocalypse Now*. Malick employs a voice-over – in this case a female one, that of the child Linda – but it hardly informs the narrative or elucidates events, let alone conveys any detailed character insight. Music tends to be privileged over dialogue, which is often unclear, and character backgrounds or motivations are barely explained so that it's hard to grasp a sense of who these people are. In 1978, the year that *Days of Heaven* won the Academy Award for Cinematography, *The Deer Hunter* won Best Film. During this decade, many film-makers were preoccupied with, or responding to, America's involvement in the Vietnam war. Malick had already done this, albeit obliquely, with his debut *Badlands* (1973) – think of the scene in the forest where Martin Sheen zig-zags predator-like through trees brandishing his gun. At the end of *Days of Heaven*, Abby boards a train with soldiers bound for action in World War One but that world feels light years away, hardly touching or impacting upon this one. It seems to be an anomaly of 70s film-making then, more akin to American literature in its reverie of innocence and experience, and the sublime; hardly naïve, its atmosphere is still ingenuous. That Malick returned fearlessly to ask crucial questions about the nature of existence through the kaleidoscope of war in *The Thin Red Line* (1998), and then dared to leave them open-ended and unanswered, is perhaps the best clue that we have.

Hannah Patterson

Blood for Dracula
(Paul Morrissey, 1974)

Paul Morrissey had barely finished *Flesh for Frankenstein* (1974) when he started filming *Blood for Dracula*, both starring European arthouse favourite, the vampy Udo Kier, and practically the same cast. Here, Andy Warhol's factory graduate - and allegedly the most square amongst the coterie of freaks that surrounded Warhol - takes us on a shambolic tour of the Italian countryside in search of virginal blood for Kier's starved vampire.

As with many Morrissey films, Warhol's name appeared as a branding strategy, but he had no real input. In fact, Warhol is indebted to Morrissey, who started his career as Warhol's assistant, in the sense that took up where the pop artist left off after he was shot and translated Warhol's formal experiments into more accessible viewing. Blood for Dracula is an alternately camp and sumptuous comedy that looks like a cross between a Penthouse soft-porn flick and landscape painting. The style elements that characterised the earlier 'collaborations' between Morrissey and Warhol are all here: amateurish camerawork, deadpan acting, dysfunctional and out-of-control personalities, long shots, and not much coherence when it comes to the script,

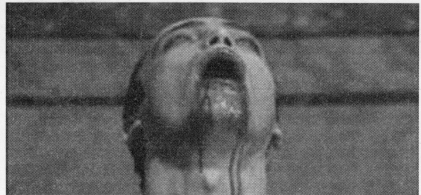

written as the film was shot.

But what could have proved fatal in an otherwise conventional film, in this playful adaptation of the classic movie monster works to its benefit and to the audience's delight. The story starts with Dracula arriving at a Tuscany-like location to scout for virgins from whom he hopes to get some much-needed blood (Morrissey made Kier lose 15 kilos for the part). On arriving in the picturesque and beautifully photographed countryside, his assistant (the perfectly cast Arno Juerging) finds out about the DiFiore family, aristocrats whose patriarch is played by Vittorio de Sica and who welcome the count in the hope of boosting their dwindling fortune. Dracula is at first smitten by the daughters, but soon enough finds out that theirs is not the virginal blood he's been craving for, thanks to the pitchfork wielding handyman Mario played by hunky Joe Dalessandro, and their own lesbian shenanigans.

The scenes where Dracula gets sick from the bad blood he drinks are absolutely stunning and Kier seems to revel in wallowing in the hammy theatricality of it all. And the grand stake-in-the-heart finale is also nothing short of memorable. Morrissey was a director who, although working in the period when auteurism was a much-favoured paradigm among film theoreticians, swam up-stream by letting go of strict directorial control. His films were free-wheeling improvisation work-outs, elsewhere described as 'slapstick neorealism', which ironically have turned Morrissey into a film author on the strength of the idiosyncratic method he conceived them by.

Blood for Dracula may not be a major legacy from the fertile arthouse cinema of the 70s, but it certainly defines a period of light-hearted experimentation, and a sense of fun that is hard to come by these days in what passes for alternative cinema. Fans of Dogme 95 and non-mainstream cinema should check it out to see where it all started.

Antonio Pasolini

"FINALLY, SOMETHING FOR EVERYONE!"
The Films of Atom Egoyan

Atom Egoyan is one of the most distinctive and acclaimed directors in world cinema today. Jason Wood, co-director of the documentary *Formulas For Seduction: The Cinema of Atom Egoyan*, talked exclusively with Egoyan on the occasion of a retrospective of his work in London earlier this year to mark the release of his latest film, *Ararat* (2002). And on page 25, Ian Haydn Smith offers an overview of Egoyan's film-making career to date.

Jason Wood: *How does it feel to look back upon a body of work that is so consistently thematically and formally challenging?*

Atom Egoyan: I really feel that I'm very much in mid-career, so the idea of a retrospective is somewhat daunting. That said, I do recognize that there are recurring obsessions and areas of fascination evident in the films. I deal with these subjects once every year or two. The viewer of a retrospective deals with them with an alarming degree of frequency.

Ararat deals with the search for sexual and cultural identity on both a

Family Viewing

collective and personal level. Those
familiar with your work will recognise
this as a theme to which you
continually return. How would you
attempt to explain the fascination this
subject holds for you?

Sexuality is a vital form of personal
expression. It involves issues of trust and
acceptance and tolerance. I'm fascinated
by sexual codes of conduct, and how they
intersect with prevailing codes of
mainstream society. *Ararat* is not so much
about the search for sexual identity, as it
is about having those identities accepted
by others.

*Similarly the film offers perhaps your
most sustained examination yet of the
ways in which we seek to validate our
experiences, histories and relationships*

*through the use of recording and
digital technology. To this is added the
notion of how art mediates our
relationship to our past. Could you say
more about the way in which you feel
this works in* **Ararat***. I was reminded
very much of* **Calendar** *(1993) in this
regard.*

Culture is based on the objects we pass on
to others. All of the Armenian characters
in the film are somehow involved in this
process of creating meaning and
significance through cultural artifacts.
From the unknown ancient architects of
the churches of Ani and Aghtamar, to the
forgotten photographer in the city of Van
taking a portrait of Gorky and his mother,
to Gorky painting his masterpiece years
later, to Ani writing a book about the
making of this masterpiece, to Rouben

writing a screenplay which will include bits of Ani's book, to Edward Saroyan filming these scenes, to Raffi finally shooting his own scene (both on mysterious film and digital video diaries), as well as telling a customs officer about what he witnessed about the making of Edward's movie. All of these characters are involved in a process of cultural transmission. In most of these cases, perceived limitations or inadequacies on the part of one teller lead to a further embellishment on the part of the next. All of the post-genocide stories are driven by a common anxiety; the anxiety of not being heard.

When we spoke previously the idea of how to approach a film telling the history of the Armenian genocide was pre-occupying you. How did you finally arrive at the complex but fascinating approach you take and what factors influenced your decision?

From the moment I began thinking of this film, I knew that any film concerning the Armenian Genocide would present certain stereotypes, and would be accused, from a Turkish perspective, of promoting hatred. Yet from an Armenian point of view – in terms of stories we have been told over and over again from the time we were children – the barbaric and vicious images were very real. The challenge in telling the story of *Ararat* was threefold: First of all, I had to find a way of presenting the strongest and most persistent of cultural beliefs with which I had been raised.

Secondly, I needed to examine and question the drives and sources that determined those beliefs. And finally, I had to show the emotional foundation of those beliefs as they persist in our culture today.

Looking back over your films I find also that the notion of fractured family relationships and the tentative attempts to re-build them is almost constant, perhaps most vividly realised in **Family Viewing** *(1987). How would you explain your interest in this theme?*

In an ideal world, families would be a matter of choice and not birth. In many of the films, the characters are driven to find new family systems which may or may not make use of blood relations. In *Ararat*, the strongest father-son link is created in the space of a few hours by two strangers who have never met before.

Ararat *perhaps represents your most deeply felt and personal work. How taxing was it to complete and given both the scale of the project, the personal resonance it has and its dealing with the Armenian Diaspora what kind of physical and emotional tolls has it taken?*

In all honesty, if I were fully aware of the overwhelming responsibility this film carried, I would have been completely paralyzed! I kept telling myself that this was an extremely personal film – my individual take on the subject. In reality, of course, it is the first and only internationally distributed film touching on the Armenian Genocide; so all Armenians have rightfully claimed it as 'theirs'. I am greatly relieved that, for the most part, they are supportive of what I have done. I needed to be true to myself, and pretended – during the production – that it was no different from my other films. This is obviously not the case. Whether or not others will see *Ararat* as my strongest or weakest film, it is undoubtedly, for Armenians, the most important.

Your work is, I feel, marked by four key collaborators: cinematographer Paul Sarossy, composer Mychael Danna, editor Susan Shipton and Arsinée Khanjian. Would you be able to comment on the creative import of these relationships?

Paul, Mychael and Susan are essential to what I do. I trust Paul completely with light, Susan to find the internal rhythm of a scene, and Mychael to add the right tone and to elaborate hidden emotions. Arsinée is the source of so much of my creative energy, and her face is an object of complete fascination. In *Ararat*, she embodies the supreme spirit of the Armenian Diaspora. The expression on her face after she walks onto the set and interrupts Bruce's extraordinary monologue is my favorite point in the film.

I think that you are at an interesting juncture in your career. What challenges and aspirations remain for you?

Like any artist, I sometimes dream of a film that 'breaks through' commercially. My problem is that I have always had final cut on my films, and couldn't dream of subjecting one of my projects to the traditional commercial/industrial system of production. My most popular film has been *Exotica* (1994), and yet I can't help but feel that this is largely due to the fact that it's set in a strip club. One day I hope to combine exotic dancers, school bus crashes, bisexual insurance adjusters, and genocide survivors in a film that has broad public appeal. I would love to have that splashed under the title of this movie, "FINALLY, SOMETHING FOR EVERYONE!"

Interview by Jason Wood

The Sweet Hereafter

Recording Memories:
Notes on the Films of
Atom Egoyan

The films of Atom Egoyan are compelling and perplexing, both digetically in terms of their narrative structure and in the way they view the world. Sidestepping genre conventions, preferring instead to concentrate on the intricacies of human relationships, his films occur at the juncture between the private and the public; where the personal – physical, psychological and sexual – reflect upon and are influenced by, the larger issues of

The Sweet Hereafter

modern society. They are a journey through a labyrinth of interconnected actions and events, each with their consequence.

With his most recent film, *Ararat*, Atom Egoyan appears to have reached a crossroads in his career. It is his realisation of a long-held ambition to confront the issues surrounding the 1915 genocide of the Armenian people at the hands of the Turkish army. Yet to even be officially recognised by the British, US and Turkish governments, the events which took place have rarely been touched upon by world cinema and certainly not as openly as Egoyan's film. And yet, *Ararat* is far from a linear re-telling. Egoyan employs his signature multiple narrative structure to question the events documented in records and personal accounts of the time, and the problems that exist in representing them. What we finally have is not a first-hand recreation of the past, but one seen through the eyes of a veteran director (*Ararat* competed for the Palme d'Or at the Cannes Film festival when Roman Polanski walked away with the award for *The Pianist* (2002), a drama that suffers from many of the problems raised in Egoyan's film), writer, actor and historical advisor, as well as more personal responses to both the genocide and how it has affected resulting generations.

Ararat is Egoyan's most personal film since 1993's *Calendar*, which features Egoyan and Arsinée Khanjian (his wife and main actor in nearly all of his work) as a photographer and his wife, whose relationship breaks down during a lengthy photo-shoot in Armenia. These scenes are juxtaposed against comical interludes back in Canada, where the now single photographer endures a series of dates with women of different nationalities. Each of these scenes ends with the woman making a phone call to their lover, talking to them in their native tongue. These moments emphasise the photographer's distance from the women in the same way that language separated him and his wife, who eventually left him for their Armenian guide. In both cases, the catalyst for this separation is technology; the telephone in his home and the video camera the photographer views the world – and his wife – through. They recall an opening moment in Egoyan's 1991 feature, *The Adjuster*. Having only just left his wife in bed, to go to work, Noah calls her on the phone to ask if she was having a bad dream, apparently unable to endure what intimacy may have arisen had he asked her at home. These scenes highlight Egoyan's fascination with memory and communication, and the part played by technology in recording, remembering and expressing.

Even from his early shorts, Egoyan displayed a fascination with recording devices and how they could be used within a narrative to examine characters' lives. His first short, *Howard in Particular*, emphasised the dehumanising side of corporate business, when an employee is despatched into retirement not by the head of the company in person, but by a recording of his voice. 1982's *Open House*

saw a more complex use of technology, in what now seems like a rehearsal for his second feature, *Family Viewing* (1987). Posing as a real estate agent, a young man shows a couple around his parents' home. As he shows them through each room, he secretively records their comments, which are played back to his mother and infirm father, creating false pride for a house that has seen better days. In *Family Viewing*, which features Egoyan's most brutal character, convincingly played by regular cast member David Hemblen, a father records over home movies of his first wife and her mother, with footage of his sexual acts with his second wife. In these films, the two main characters attempt to the return to or erase the past with the present. In both cases, that attempt fails.

Egoyan's first feature, *Next of Kin* (1984) stands alone from his other films for its sheer simplicity and directness. Patrick Tierney plays Peter Foster, a young man whose apparent lack of emotional engagement with his family is a cause for concern for his parents. Following a video recorded appointment with a therapist and a resulting mix-up of tapes, Peter finds himself watching footage of an Armenian couple, whose troubled relationship with their adult daughter appears to stem from the guilt over the son they were forced to give up, shortly after arriving in Canada. Posing as the son, Peter enters a domestic environment that proves to be the antithesis of his own family experience. In the film's pivotal scene, he delivers a speech to his new family, expressing his happiness at being able to choose the family he wants to live with. His real parents are left with a recording of his voice, expressing his happiness at finally having become part of a family he can communicate with.

The themes that Egoyan explored in his first three films have continued to play a part in his work. However, the early 1990's saw a broadening of his canvas. *The Adjuster* now seems something of a watershed in terms of Egoyan's career. It is certainly the bridge between his earlier and more recent work. The recording device, both audio and visual, maintains a prominent place within the narrative. But what marks *The Adjuster* as one of Egoyan's most satisfying works is the sheer complexity of the narrative and the confidence with which he brings it to the screen. The first of his 'jigsaw' narratives, which continue through *The Sweet Hereafter* (1997), *Exotica* and *Ararat*, it is an enigmatic and frequently unsettling film. Egoyan stated that he 'wanted to make a film about believable people doing believable things in an unbelievable way'. At the centre of these stories is Noah Render, an insurance adjuster who compensates his inability to communicate with anyone intimately with his extraordinary generosity to his clients, whose homes or places of work have been destroyed. Housing them in a local motel – a makeshift ark that befits his name – whose staff worship him, Noah goes to any lengths to recreate the experience of home, be it replicating a favourite room of proffering sexual favours, be they male or female. His wife is also an adjuster, but in cultural terms. As a film censor, she judges what is right for society to watch. However, in order for her non-English speaking sister to understand her role and her place in society, she records the excised scenes of sex and violence on a hidden video recorder. It is only when they are approached by a wealthy couple posing as film-makers and are asked if their house can be used as a location for a shoot, forcing them into the motel inhabited by Noah's clients, that they realise how maladjusted their lives really are, leading to the inevitable disintegration of their relationship and family.

Both *Exotica* and *The Sweet Hereafter* mine a similar territory of fragmented lives. These films are imbued with a sense of loss for the past; of a time that can never be regained and as a result, only those willing to learn from the events they have experienced can move on with their lives. *The Sweet Hereafter* displays this sense of loss most overtly, in terms of the deaths of the children on the school bus and Mitch Steven's relationship with his daughter. Only Nicole, whose accident-induced paralysis has enlightened her relationship with her father, has gained in some way since the tragedy. The survivor of the Pied Piper's story, which she narrates throughout the film (an inspired addition to Egoyan's adaptation of Russell Banks' novel), she mourns the loss of her friends, but is wiser for her experience.

Only time will tell if *Ararat* marks a new stage in Egoyan's career. It certainly sees a return to his tapestry-like approach to film-making, after the linear – aside of the flashbacks to the central character's past – adaptation of William Trevor's *Felicia's Journey* (1999). For some critics however, *Ararat* was a disappointment, lacking Egoyan's usual subtlety. Certainly, there are problems in attempting to present history whilst simultaneously questioning the feasibility of its cinematic representation. But what marks *Ararat* out is Egoyan's willingness to deal with personal issues. In an age where globalisation within cinema has resulted in the marketing of films that appeal to the most diverse audience, the cinema of Atom Egoyan stands out not only for its complexity and intelligence, but also for the director's willingness to confront his own feelings about the world around him.

Ian Haydn Smith

TRANS-EUROPEAN EXCESS

The 21st Brussels International Festival of Fantastic Films

For followers of the fantastic, Belgium has a long and important tradition that exceeds its historic links with painting, surrealism and the creative arts. This is because for the last 21 years, its capital has been host to one of Europe's most prestigious genre film events: the spectacular **International Festival of Fantasy, Thriller and Science Fiction Film**, which is held annually in March. Unlike many genre based festivals, the Brussels festival makes a conscious decision not to differentiate the 'fantastic' as being limited to any one genre, but instead focuses on celebrating the very best upcoming releases from a variety of film formats. As a result, the festival attracts nightly audiences of well over 900 people for its main screening venue,

Auditorium 44, as well as an additional 200 attendants for the special retrospectives held nightly at its sister location: Nova Cinema. The festival programmes fantasy films from a variety of regions, with strong European, American and far Eastern traditions being represented. As well as judging the fantastic in a variety of non-cinematic art forms (such as painting, poster and body art as well as literature), the festival organisers recently took the innovative step of including multimedia/gaming formats as part of their annual remit.

Guests at the festival frequently appear to promote forthcoming works or to oversee special retrospectives, and this year attendants included Danny Boyle, Alex Cox, Eli Roth, Bob Gale, Vincenzo Natali and Brian Yuzna. Also present were Alejandro Jodorowksy (who presided over a special retrospective of his works such as *El Topo* (1970) and *Holy Mountain* (1973)) as well as cult British director Richard Stanley, who staged a film-makers workshop for students and interns.

European Connections

With a series of network connections spreading across of a number of related festivals in neighbouring countries, it is not surprising that European movies featured heavily in both the premiere and retrospective strands of the Brussels

Beyond Re-animator

International Fantasy Festival. This year, entrants included the French supernatural prison movie *Malefique*, a stark Croatian ghost story entitled *The Sunken Cemetery* and even an interesting British trench-horror movie *Death Watch*, which was directed by Michael J. Bassett.

Beyond the wealth of European productions on show at the festival, what was also evident was the increasingly transnational nature that genre film-making is adopting in the face of high budget Hollywood competition. While this degree of co-operation has always existed *between* European countries, it is also witnessing major US fantasy film-makers relocating to Europe to take advantage of these structures. One such director is Brian Yuzna, the creator of such gore classics as *Society* (1989), *The Dentist* (1996) and *Return of the Living Dead Part III* (1993). In 2000, Yuzna and prolific Spanish producer Julio Fernandez formed the Fantastic Factory, with the intention of creating an outfit able to draw on leading acting and production talents from around the world. As Yuzna is a self confessed European horror fan, it seemed appropriate that he fully immerse in such a film-making culture and he has since relocated his family and film-making activities totally to Spain. The Fantastic Factory have already produced several films with Yuzna in both directorial and production roles. These have included *Faust* (2000), an updated cult comic book version of the man who sold his soul to the devil and *Araknid* (2001), a scary spider extravaganza directed by Jack

Shoulder. As well as show-casing a number of Fantastic Factory films which he had produced, Yuzna also premiered his latest instalment of the Herbert West saga, *Beyond Re-Animator*, at the festival. This sequel to the 1980s horror classic finds the mad scientist West incarcerated in a prison for his crimes, though he still cannot resist dabbling with body parts and the living dead. With the Yuzna trademark features of excessive gore punctuated with moments of dark, dark humour *Beyond Re-Animator* was an instant crowd-pleaser, confirming the director's Fantastic Factory venture as one of the most exciting projects to evolve in genre film-making for quite a while.

The Feel-Good Fantastic

As well as providing an ideal platform for emerging European productions, the Brussels 21st International Festival of Fantastic Films continued its tradition of promoting forthcoming American releases that transcend the mainstream and independent divide. As a result, this year's Stateside suitors demonstrated an eclectic mix of works that both confirmed as well as challenged what we expect from genre film-making.

For instance, although the festival often trades on images of gore and nihilistic excess, one surprise hit was Bob Gale's directorial debut *Interstate 60*. Best known for creating the *Back to the Future* series with Robert Zemekis, Gale's movie is an endearing and uplifting study that uses the mythology of the American open-road as a metaphor for the life choices a young

man faces during his journey into adulthood. In the film, Neal Oliver (James Marsden) wrestles with his dreams of becoming an artist while at the same time trying to keep his overbearing father's desire for him to become a lawyer at bay. When it looks as though the patriarch may win out, Neal's dreams are saved following a 'chance' encounter with the eccentric waiter O.W. Grant (Gary Oldman), who is revealed as a wish-giver with magical powers. Grant sends the young boy on an errand through an interstate that does not exist, across the towns that America has either forgotten or failed to acknowledge, in order for him to realise what he really wants out of life.

While *Interstate 60*, clearly works as a 'rights of passage' movie, it also manages to maintain the sly digs at corporate American culture often found in Gale's writing. This is most clearly seen in the nightmarish sequence where the hero is forced to journey through one American town where every citizen is suing their neighbour and innocent people are arrested in order to create more work for money hungry lawyers. Although the scene is played for laughs, it is clearly intended as a comment on the excesses of litigation culture so prevalent within the United States. While these comic encounters ensure that *Interstate 60* remains an amusing tale, the film also benefits from some wonderful cameo appearances that clearly reference Gale's past work (and his associations with the Zemeckis/Spielberg stable). Thus, Kurt (*Used Cars*) Russell is cast as the ponytailed Sheriff of a town that sanctions teenage drug-taking in return for domestic subservience, while Christopher Lloyd pops up as a crack pot benefactor, clearly recalling his 'mad inventor' role from *Back to the Future*. The link to this latter film is also confirmed by a brief but wonderfully executed cameo from Michael J. Fox, here cast as an uptight company executive who falls fatally foul of his wish not to have his cell-phone destroyed by an encounter with O.W. Grant.

A Pact of Death

While *Interstate 60* keeps its fantasy in a feel-good mood, the same can not be said of many of the other American entrants at this year's Brussels festival. For instance, *Emmett's Mark* is a melancholic and brooding movie from first time director Keith Snyder. The film juxtaposes a young detective's hunt for a serial killer stalking local women with his discovery of the degenerative and fatal brain disorder threatening his own life. Rather than endure a slow and lingering demise, Emmett (Scott Wolf) strikes up a bizarre deal with the mysterious ex-cop Marlow (Gabriel Byrne), who arranges for a hit man to assassinate the young detective at an unknown point in the next three days. However, when Emmett discovers that his fatal illness is in fact a misdiagnosis, he finds himself caught in a deadly game of cat and mouse, unable to contact Marlow and terminate the contract that will effectively cancel his own life. With edgy, Fincher-like camerawork and strong character performances from Wolf, Byrne and Tim Roth (as the reluctant hitman), the film deals with introspective characters whose greatest fear is the thought of dying unloved and alone. *Emmett's Mark* is in many respects a-typical of the kind of movies that populate genre festivals, but it is a thought provoking and intense film from an emerging new American director.

Whose Reality?

Far less moody than *Emmett's Mark,* but just as disturbing is *Cypher*, the long-awaited new movie from *Cube* (1997) visionary Vincenzo Natali. In the film, an out of work accountant Morgan Sullivan (Jeremy Northam) accepts a job as a company spy for the sinister conglomerate

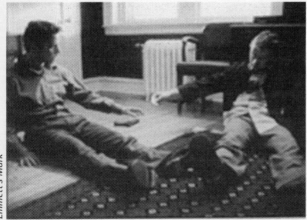
Emmett's Mark

Digicorp. This results in him having to adopt a new identity in order to report back to his new employer on a series of seemingly innocent business conventions. However, at one such conference, he encounters the seductive Rita (Lucy Liu), who works as an agent for Digicorp's main business rival. Rita informs Sullivan that Digicorp are in fact brainwashing him in order to steal his original identity. Armed with (yet another) new identity, Sullivan attempts to turn the tables on his employers by acting as a double agent who is secretly passing on information to Rita's organisation. With its play on the theme of male characters whose sense of reality and established identity is undercut, *Cypher* fits perfectly with the current vogue for 'cine-psychosis' found in contemporary American cinema. The director's trademark frenzied visual style adds polish to this theme, particularly in the scenes where Sullivan experiences flashbacks in the form of rapid MTV style inserts. *Cypher* proved a firm favourite with festival audiences and looks like doing the same with British viewers when it hits the UK later this year.

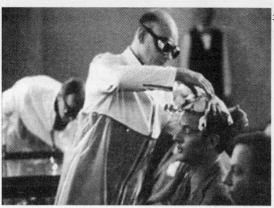

Cypher

Crazed Country Cousins

With such a wealth of exciting new films on offer, choosing a favourite is always a difficult task. However, the two films that impressed me the most at this year's festival were *Cabin Fever* and *May*, both contemporary examples of the American underground cinema. Eli Roth's *Cabin Fever* depicts the grisly fate of a group of five young city dwellers who decide to spend the final days of their college vacation in a remote, country log cabin. However, this rural location harbours a much more deadly threat than just the backward and barbaric locals that populate the location. As the film reveals, the region's water supply has been subjected to chemical contamination by hapless authorities. Those unfortunate enough to drink from this source become infected by a flesh eating virus that provokes lesions to erupt through the skin's surface, before madness, irrational acts of violence and fatal decomposition occur. With its visceral visualisation of physical decay, *Cabin Fever* will undoubtedly prove shocking to some viewers used to 'sanitised' vision of horror that continues to dominate mainstream images of the genre. However, what makes Roth's film truly disturbing is the lack of humanity that characters display towards the sick and infected depicted in the film. For instance, when one elderly local strays into the youngsters camp seeking medical assistance, he is first warded off with warning shots before the group set him on fire and leave his body burning in the nearby woods.

As this brief description of *Cabin Fever* indicates, the film is an extremely downbeat production that is strongly reminiscent of the most nihilistic horror movies of 1970s. Indeed, the comparison with seventies American horror is no coincidence, as scenes from *Cabin Fever* make clear Roth's debt to directors such as Tobe Hooper, Wes Craven and George A. Romero. The film's depiction of amoral and lethal country bumpkins clearly echo representations found in notorious seventies productions such as *The Texas Chainsaw Massacre* (1974). Equally, it's focus on the mindless violence that accompanies the clash of city and country cultures is derived from Wes Craven's controversial debut movie *The Last House on the Left* (1973). The influence of the latter production on Roth's own development is underscored by the fact that he even re-mixes David Hess' haunting soundtrack for *Last House on the Left* into key scenes of *Cabin Fever*, while the cinematography also closely mirrors the visual style of Craven's rape and revenge drama. In marked opposition to the current trends in Beverly Hills horrors, Eli Roth has consciously rejected the self-reflexive, silly and ultimately safe brand of genre movie that has dominated the post-*Scream* (1996) arena. Instead, his film is a stark vision of a culture's manifest inhumanity that is uncompromising, intense and intelligent.

May's Eye for Horror

Coming a close second to Roth's masterful debut is Lucky McKee's genuinely unsettling film *May*. The movie concerns a social misfit, ostracised since childhood because of an imperfection with one of her eyes. Seeking solace and company in her mother's home-made doll, May enters adult life introverted and unbalanced.

Cabin Fever

When she meets a local mechanic with an obsession for Dario Argento films, it looks as though her link with normality is finally assured. However, with the deep sense of impending doom that permeates the movie, it is only a matter of time before she realises that her physical and mental peculiarities have made her the ultimate laughing stock within her community. Having been rejected by her boyfriend as 'too weird' and having been spurned by one potential lesbian suitor in favour of an all-American cupcake girl, May's final link to sanity is shattered when her beloved doll is destroyed by the kids at the local blind school where she works. Out of desperation, May creates a second and even more perfect companion: using the body parts of the people who have tormented her. With *May*, the director is clearly updating the classic tale of *Frankenstein*, as well as paying homage to prom-horror classics such as *Carrie*. What makes McKee's film so interesting is the fact that traditional Gothic themes are transposed onto a white-trash, working-class setting, while the camerawork and character interactions recall the off-centre concerns of Indie icons such as Kevin Smith. This fusion of the classic and contemporary ensures that the final twenty minutes of McKee's movie is a whacked-out bloodbath with body bits and bitching taking centre stage. Topped off by an outstanding performance by

May

Angela Bettis as the painfully shy lead character, *May* ushers in a new horror heroine for the slacker generation.

As usual, the 21st Brussels International Festival has provided an unbeatable perfect platform for all the latest global developments in fantastic cinema. With plans for an aligned conference around the theme of European Trash cinema already in development, next year's event promises to be even more significant.

Xavier Mendik

With thanks to Christoph Foque, Dirk Van Extergem, Thibaut Dopchie, Marie-France Dupagne and all the staff at the Brussels International Festival of Fantastic Film for their assistance and hospitality during the Cult Film Archive's 2003 visit.

RECLAIM THE SCREENS
Why short films need to be seen

In the first of his regular columns about the short film scene, Mathieu Ravier argues that the time has come for a radical re-thinking of the distribution and exhibition of shorts.

The first film ever made was a short. Over a century later, thousands of short films are still produced around the world each year. Most established film-makers working today started with short-form work, some return to the format then and, again, others have no plans to ever abandon it. Production seems to have reached an all-time high and shows no sign of decreasing, helped along by the affordability of user-friendly digital video. Yet general audiences are not very familiar with the format. Beyond ads and music videos, short films seem to remain below the radar of collective consciousness. Distributors and exhibitors shy away from the format, film critics are mostly silent on the subject while cultural policy sometimes tends to ignore shorts altogether. There is cause for concern: short films play a vital role in the global film-making process. Raising their profile would not only benefit the film industry but ensure that well-made films reach the audience they deserve.

Supporting short directors makes sense: they are tomorrow's film industry. With lower costs and less pressure to deliver work that can turn a profit at the box-office, short films act as a petri dish where new approaches and techniques are tested. The variety of formats, media and styles at its disposal – from DV to 35mm, from live action to animation, from traditional narrative to experimental work – make shorts a playground for the adventurous. Innovation is the most significant by-product of short film production. This is hugely significant for the global film industry which needs to constantly renew itself creatively and technically, but won't take the risks involved in doing so. We cannot complain endlessly about the UK film industry churning out formulaic romantic comedies, uninspired gangster thrillers and cheap horror films and continue to ignore the wealth of original ideas lying dormant in the unseen bulk of short film production.

Shorts, besides, are not just student exercises or the first drafts of feature-length projects. Like the short story, the short film can be considered an art form in its own right, and should be enjoyed and valued as such. Innovative, entertaining or thought-provoking shorts such as Luis Buñuel's *Un Chien Andalou*, Chris Marker's *La Jetée* and even Nick Park's *Creature Comforts* have become classics to rival their more expensive, widely-distributed feature-film counterparts. The early short films of Martin Scorcese, George Lucas or Ridley Scott are arguably more inspired than their recent work. First films by Jane Campion, Krzysztof Kieslowski or Jean-Pierre Jeunet are undoubtedly accomplished works which manifest the talent, style and thematic interests present in their feature films. The latter trio of film-makers had the chance to make their first films in countries that (at the time) mostly nurtured their film-makers with supportive cultural policies. Let's hope that such attention is paid to the short film-makers from Brazil, Mexico and Scandinavia - whose current crop is nothing short of exceptional - and to short film-makers in the UK, who need all the help they can get.

The commercial sector's reluctance to embrace the format is mostly down to shorts' apparent lack of marketability. Shorts can rarely afford stars or special effects, and they suffer from the same hostile climate which threatens the survival of arthouse cinema in general. Raising the quality and profile of short films is an imperative which – in the UK - has been somewhat ignored by film critics, policy makers and educators alike.

Very little is written about shorts. The recent *In Short – A Guide to Short Film-making in the Digital Age* (Eileen Elsey & Andrew Kelly, BFI Publishing) was the first book published on the subject in this country in years. By contrast, shorts have their own glossy magazine in France ('Bref'), whose readership extends beyond practitioners.

Another obstacle to many profile-raising exercises is the sheer volume of shorts produced each year. Digital film-making has recently opened up the practise to a much wider and more diverse population. Toronto's Worldwide Short Film Festival, though only in its third year, had to field over 2300 entries for its June

2003 event. Suffice to say, much filtering needs to be done if we are to get audiences interested. This is where film festivals (and the distinctions they bestow) come in. There are over 1000 film festivals in the world, many of whom include short films in their line-ups. Collectively, they sift through countless films, offering the best for general consumption. In the era of the multiplex, when arthouse cinemas are constantly fighting for survival or going mainstream to compete, festivals are fast becoming the new exhibition sector for arthouse films – often the sole exhibitors in the case of shorts. A high price could be paid if policy makers and funders continue to underestimate the role Festivals play in showcasing shorts, nurturing film-makers and celebrating diversity.

Film-makers, in turn, should be encouraged to make *better* shorts. For that to happen, funders need to better understand the format and adapt their policies accordingly. The priority should be funding the best projects – wherever they may come from – rather than those who 'tick' the most boxes. Funding bodies' approach to project selection is ironically as formulaic as that of commercial studios, and too many film-makers let funding criteria dictate the films they want to make. Equally, more emphasis should be put on education and training, particularly in the area of script development, which only a handful of short film-makers resort to.

Better shorts might help overcome the biggest obstacle to the recognition that short films deserve: distribution. Short films rarely get distributed, despite the array of formats in which they can be screened. The stakes are high for shorts to screen in cinemas: these high profile screenings have a positive knock-on effect on other formats such as video and television.

Traditionally, feature film distribution starts with theatrical release, usually followed by video and DVD, ending with television broadcast. Shorts can follow a similar pattern and be screened before features or as part of special thematic programmes. Programmes such as the recent *09'11"01*, which featured shorts about September 11th made by established film-makers, are one way to market shorts to a theatrical audience. The likely advent of digital cinemas in the UK could open up more screens to short-form work, significantly lowering the cost of prints. But in spite of these possibilities, shorts will not get shown without the backing of strong political will. Screening shorts before features incurs additional costs while the box-office potential of the add-ons is unproven. Until the theatrical distribution and exhibition of short films are intelligently subsidized, there is little cause for optimism. For the time being we can only dream about such projects as Cine Alternatif, a Parisian cinema which was set up to screen mostly short films.

More effort is also needed to bring short films to the attention of broadcasters. The boom in cable and satellite channels means that the demand for content is at an all-time high.

Intelligently packaged thematic programmes could be a welcome addition to a channel's grid, and a logical choice for a public broadcaster with a clear mandate. Now that the hype has died down, it is a good time to study the real potential of on-line webcasting of short films. DVD is also a format that offers new avenues for short film distribution. Short film compilations such as the *Cinema 16* DVDs promise to be popular and hopefully viable products. Recently shorts like the BAFTA winning *My Wrongs 8245-8249 and 117* have been released on DVD, very much in the manner of CD singles. It is also increasingly frequent for shorts by the same film-maker to be added as 'extras' on feature DVD releases.

Film festivals remain the primary outlets for short film distribution today. At a time of popcorn blockbusters and mind-numbing television, shorts can be an acquired taste. Festivals are great places to sample these rare delights and learn about the films from the film-makers themselves. Events such as the Clermont International Short Film Festival in France, with attendance equal to its host city's population (135,000), prove that the audience for shorts, if nurtured, can achieve critical mass. Free, outdoor short film nights such as Silhouette in Paris or the infamous Tropfest in Australia, which draws 160,000 spectators each year, are another popular way to showcase the films.

Finally, distributors have a duty to explore new, original ideas for exhibition. Interfilm in Berlin have run 'Going Underground' for over two years now. The project involves screening short films in the Berlin underground (U-bahn lines 5, 6, 7, 8 and 9), exposing the film to an audience of 2 million viewers! New business models can be investigated to make short film exhibition viable in outlets as diverse as hospital waiting rooms, airplanes, airports and even mobile phones.

The impact of wider distribution of short films is far-reaching and should not be underestimated. If the originality and vitality of British short film production were to percolate into feature film production and be factored into audience expectations, we could end up with healthier, more vibrant film industry.

Mathieu Ravier

What's Up, Docs?

Interest in documentary film is at its highest in years. Increasing numbers of film students are working in the medium; more television outlets need documentary product for their schedules; and the theatrically-released documentary has been given a huge boost by the success of two films in the last year alone – *Lost in La Mancha* and, especially, *Bowling for Columbine* (both 2002). In the first of his columns for KAMERA, documentary film-maker and lecturer Searle Kochberg looks at the changing climate for documentary film.

Something is in the air. Growing numbers of people are choosing to see documentaries in a theatrical setting, away from the delights of the box. Many of us are putting our money down to see documentaries at general film festivals, where non fiction film is amongst the most popular: still a little way behind (fiction) feature film, but up there with experimental film and animation. In the specialist festival market, the two largest documentary festivals - the International Documentary Film Festival Amsterdam (November each year) and Hot Docs in Toronto (May) - are growing in popularity every year. Figures for the 2002 IDFA event attest to this: attendance records are at 70,000, and around 200 films were screened.

Those pundits who have followed the

growing success of theatrical exhibition of documentaries over the last decade are aware that "Documentary Features" have led the way in this phenomenon. The Doc Feature category has cleverly built on the platform afforded it at festivals and gone on to successful multiple runs in mainstream multiplexes. Films that spring to mind include Michael Moore's *Roger and Me* (1989), Jennie Livingston's *Paris is Burning* (1990), Steve James's *Hoop Dreams* (1994), Leon Gast's *When We Were Kings* (1996), Wim Wenders' *Buena Vista Social Club* (1998), and most recently Moore's *Bowling for Columbine* (2002). These titles are labelled "documentary features" not only because of their length, but also because of their clear emphasis on plot (strong narrative drive, engaging protagonists). In other words, a documentary feature is more than just a feature-length documentary: the label also implies a documentary that aspires to a structure not dissimilar to a Hollywood film. It's easy therefore to speculate on the reason for the doc film's theatrical success: it meets the marketing criteria of sales agents/distributors around the world and the expectations of film audiences. In other words, it ties in to everyone's expectations of "a night at the movies."

But why are less obviously commercial documentaries also growing in popularity with theatrical audiences today? To answer this question we really need to look at the changing nature of TV commissioning since the inception of cable/satellite.

In his essay, 'What's in store...the future of auteur documentary'[1], Jan Rofekamp, President of Films Transit (sales agents for documentaries), speaks for many when he argues that the increase in 'thematic' (i.e. specialist) cable and satellite channels throughout the '90s, such as the Discovery Channel, built new audiences for documentaries. However, it also led to the commissioning of cheaper programming across the TV sector in general. The move to digital production only exacerbated the situation by creating a climate of ever increasing amounts of Z-grade reality TV programming. Meanwhile, the new audiences, fed up with a ceaseless diet of reality TV on the networks and cable, turned to festivals to provide more thought-provoking, independent, less official views of the world.

Rofekamp would be the first to admit, however, that it would be unfair to trash the TV sector completely. As he argues, TV is still a home for new directions in documentary because creative makers, driven sales agents (such as he) and enlightened commissioning groups (such as NPS in Holland, ZDF in Germany, ARTE in France, Channel 4 in the UK and PBS in the U.S.) continue to defend 'authored' documentary (i.e. the creative, independent documentary marked by the style of its maker).

Whatever the follies of current commissioning, TV companies have clearly cottoned on to benefits of festivals for building audiences prior to broadcast. They use festivals to launch their product with reviewers and to raise the profile of their programmes with the public. This process of indirect publicity is different from dedicated industry sales events (like the huge MIP-TV market in Cannes every summer), and is in evidence at all major festivals attended by the public. For instance, at the 2003 Human Rights Film Festival in London, the BBC launched two of its documentaries from the current affairs series, *Correspondent*.

Away from the mainstream world of documentary marketing and exhibition, film and video artists are now crossing the boundaries between documentary, experimental film and narrative fiction cinema. This type of work rarely gets an airing on TV. But, its outings elsewhere – in theatres, on the web, etc. – have allowed the cultural framework in which documentary work is traditionally understood to shift, to widen. The work of Jem Cohen is a good example of this. In the 2001 screening of his work at London's National Film Theatre, works such as *Lost Book Found* (1996) and *Blood Orange Sky* (1999) were screened. The first film melds documentary and fiction narrative into a complex dialogue on city life, ephemera and the *flaneur*. In his own words, Cohen creates 'an archive of undirected shots and sounds... [and] then set[s] out to explore the boundary' between genres.[2] In the second film/video, Cohen offers a visual/sound portrait of Catania, Sicily, with music by Mark Linkous and local Catanian musicians.

The low cost of digital production has also stimulated other creative initiatives,

resulting in crossover projects that also build new audiences for non-fiction in a theatrical/concert setting. Increasingly, an MTV generation of creative practitioners is recognising the potential of music and film/video collaborations. Take a group such as the Yeast collective as an example. It was established in London in 1999 to foreground environmental issues through media/new media. Apart from making conventional broadcast documentary (such as *Global Protest: the Battle of Prague*, BBC, 2000), the group has run its own film nights of experimental and socially aware work, and mounts projections of visuals in art galleries, clubs and festivals. One of Yeast's ongoing collaborative areas is the production of image-tracks to compliment live concert performance. This type of collaboration has been recorded by Yeast in its crossover film of the *Nitin Sawhney World Tour* (2001). The non-fiction film weaves together Sawhney's album, 'Prophesy', and a music video format, fashioning what I perceive as a new hybridised form. The project creates a sound/image performative experience for punters, but at the same time touches upon traditional themes of 'hard' documentary, by dealing with the subjects of indigenous peoples, colonialism, and the public's understanding of the term 'development'.

The low cost of digital video (DV) has also afforded self funding groups the opportunity to make and screen works for specialist audiences. Take, for instance, the work of Globalise Resistance which utilises new media technologies to construct polemical documentaries from the perspective of the anti-globalisation movement - a perspective that Globalise Resistance feels is not represented adequately by commercial media organisations (even by Yeast!). Streaming media and mini DV cameras allow spokespersons from this anti-globalisation movement to make their case in videos such as *Genoa Libera* (2000): their record of the G8 summit. Theatrical exhibition of the work is made possible through the support of groups such as the Documentary Film-makers Group, London, which arranges public screenings at venues such as the London Film School. As in the earlier cases cited above, new creative voices, new technologies and new audiences are giving the documentary genre and its exhibition a much-needed shot in the arm.

This is an exciting time to be working in and consuming non-fiction product.

Theatrical venues are more than ever playing their part in building new audiences for new types of documented experience. However, other distribution windows will also have to play their part if the new directions are to be consolidated. It is still far too difficult to see innovative international documentary on video/DVD or on any national terrestrial station. I suggest enlightened commissioning editors and buyers spend more time fighting for new product, for with it comes new audiences: their life blood.

Searle Kochberg

1   first printed in *DOX Documentary Film Magazine*, December 2000, and available online at www.nfb.ca/documentary/html/en/2.4.1 e-whats_in_store.html
2   quoted in NFT programme notes from "Programme 2: Later days," dated 3/2/01.

André Bazin

Kamera aspires to bi-monthly bulletins of quality writing about the movies. Yet good writing about film, *really* good writing, is too often a contradictory concept. In the mainstream media a 'film reviewer' is one who describes a plot then awards a film marks out of five; in more rarefied literary circles, being able to write eloquently about the defining art form of the twentieth century is too often seen as slumming it.

In this regular column, Richard Armstrong (who reviews the recent book, *Writers on Film*, in our Books section) will each issue investigate a great writer of film criticism and their lasting influence. He begins with the founder of *Cahiers du cinema*.

André Bazin is the most influential writer on the cinema in the post war period. A practicing critic who wrote widely but never formulated a theory, his work on the ontological properties of the image not only mounted a serious challenge to the orthodoxy of Soviet Formalism but laid the foundations of auteurism and informed the emergence of the French New Wave.

He was born in Angers, France on 18 April 1918. Studying to be a teacher, he was refused a certificate owing to a stammer and poor health. Always a lover of film, during the Second World War he established a cine-club showing banned films in defiance of the Nazi occupation. At a postwar moment of huge public interest in the cinema, Bazin took films into factories, trade union halls and cine-clubs. His name is key to the development of the cine-club movement. Contributing to publications including *Le Parisien libéré*, in 1947 Bazin started *La Revue du cinéma*. In 1951 he founded *Cahiers du cinéma* with Jacques Doniol-Valcroze and Giuseppe LoDuca, which is now one of the most respected film journals in the world. In the 1950s Bazin taught at the French national film school, IDHEC (Institut des Hautes Études Cinématographiques).

Bazin's chief contribution to

contemporary film theory was his appreciation of the revelatory nature of the photographic image. When the camera is pointed at a scene it captures and preserves part of nature. Film records the rich continuum of space and time as it happens. Bazin brought all the passion and intellectual rigour of Catholic philosophy and socialist commitment to the case for cinematic realism, the camera's revelations having a moral as well as an aesthetic dimension. 'The cinema more than any other art is bound up with love,' he wrote, celebrating a meditative relationship between lens and nature, his early training in phenomenology acknowledging the shared nature of our knowledge of the world. Yet the lens is not an uncomplicated mirror on the world for Bazin. He invokes the mathematical asymptote, that line that continually approaches a given curve but never meets it, to describe the relationship between image and object. Documentaries and scientific films were the purest forms of cinema because they deliberately foreground the camera's objectivity, its proper relationship with reality. (It is worth remembering that the French term for lens is 'objectif').

Able as a journalist to respond quickly to new movements, for Bazin Italian Neo-Realism represented the most valid expression of filmic truth. Responding to the blend of verisimilitude and compassion that he saw there, the critic hailed works such as *Paisá* (1946), *Bicycle Thieves* (1948) and *Umberto D* (1952) for revealing the very being of post war urban life. Of *Bicycle Thieves*, he writes: "Its true meaning lies in not betraying the essence of things, in allowing them first to exist for their own sakes, freely; it is to love them in their single individual reality. 'My little sister reality', says De Sica, and she circles about him like the birds around St. Francis. Others put her in a cage or teach her to talk, but De Sica talks to her and it is the true language of reality that we hear, the word that cannot be denied, that only love can express."

Related to the neo-realist revelation of nature is Bazin's appreciation of mise-en-scène. Again, the term is invested with almost mystical regard for the unfolding of space and time. If Soviet montage theory had become the theoretical orthodoxy, mise-en-scène recalled the 'photogénie' and automatism of the displaced Impressionist and Surrealist schools. Such terms stressed the ineffability of the image, its ability to be present but resist, exceed definition. For Bazin, the proper organization of space could generate a sublime supplement, what US critic Andrew Sarris later saw as a serendipitous tension between the studio auteur and his material. Preserving the spatio-temporal continuity of the scene, mise-en-scène freed the spectator from the didactic spectacle of constructed meaning that occurred in Soviet style editing. Bazin championed directors like Stroheim, Flaherty, Murnau and Renoir for their revelation of a space the spectator is free to explore. Of Stroheim, Bazin wrote: 'reality lays itself bare like a suspect confessing under the relentless examination of the commissioner of police.'

For Bazin, the development of deep focus lenses and their use in Hollywood in the prewar period signalled the emergence of a 'post-classical' aesthetic in American cinema in which the strictly narrative compulsion of Hollywood continuity editing gave way to the accumulation of meaning in the single shot. Whilst continuity editing tended to make time mental and abstract, mise-en-scène and the sequence shot (or 'plan-Américain') combined the revelation of space with real time and duration. Bazin's writings on Welles and Wyler particularly catch the transition from a flat programme-based aesthetic to a cinema of density and allusion. In 1948 Bazin felt that, along with *Paisá*, '*Citizen Kane* was the most significant event in the evolution of the cinema. *Citizen Kane* can never be too highly praised. Thanks to the depth of field, whole scenes can be covered in one take, the camera remaining motionless.' Bazin often comes back to Wyler's ascetic editing style and feeling for space. 'Between them, director and cameraman have converted the screen into a dramatic checkerboard, planned down to the last detail. The clearest if not the most original examples of this are to be found in *The Little Foxes* (1941) where the mise-en-scène takes on the severity of a working drawing.'

Bazin's feeling for mise-en-scène was a major influence upon the auteurist bent of his disciples at *Cahiers du cinéma*.

Francois Truffaut considered Bazin to be 'intelligence itself', dedicating his first film – *Les Quatre Cents Coups* (1959) – to him. But whilst Bazin admired 'the genius of the system,' he was quick to criticise the indiscriminate canonization of Hollywood auteurs and their works. Bazin's legacy, however, can still be felt in every writer with a developed sensitivity to mise-en-scène. His crisp accounts of Hollywood aesthetics in essays *The Evolution of the Language of Cinema* and *The Evolution of the Western* continue to inform contemporary notions of Hollywood 'classicism'.

Sadly, Bazin died in 1958 just as the New Wave that he sponsored was being born. Bazin brought humanist compassion combined with scientific rigour to film writing, practically inventing its literary project. Describing in intimate detail the shifting dynamic as a little boy realises that his father is not a god in *Bicycle Thieves* on the one hand, on the other Bazin's logic can be reminiscent of a laboratory log in which a thesis is stated, denied, a fresh thesis is proved. Writer after writer has noted the rich deployment of figure and example from a wealth of disciplines. As James Monaco has written: 'for the first time film theory becomes not a matter of pronouncement and prescription, but a fully mature intellectual activity, well aware of its own limitations. The very title of Bazin's collected essays (What is Cinema?) reveals the modesty of this approach. For Bazin, the questions are more important than the answers.' If Francois Mitry challenged the objectivity of the image, and others at *Cahiers du cinéma* labelled his apolitical aesthetics bourgeois and masculinist in the politicised 1970s, Bazin's preoccupation with representation looms over contemporary writing on the ethics of the image. Bazin's sponsorship of film commentary as a form of literature seems to have been borne out by Roland Barthes who in 1973 wrote "Let the commentary itself be a text. There are no more critics, only writers." One can even detect in Bazin's 1946 analysis of that American imperialist icon the Pin-Up Girl a hint of that key 1970s semiotics text Barthes', *Mythologies*. It is fitting that the practicing film critic's auteurist legacy should be reproduced, albeit in diluted condition, in contemporary mainstream film journalism, if a pity that a male bias continues to infect it.

Richard Armstrong

Books

Every issue *Kamera* will bring you reviews of the most notable of recent publications on film. We assume that if you have bought *Kamera* you appreciate good writing on the subject and want to find out more. From academic Film Studies to gossipy biographies, you can read about the best (and, perhaps, sometimes the worst) film books here.

**Stars and Masculinities
in Spanish Cinema**
Chris Perriam
£35.00, 019815996X,
Oxford University Press

If, as is widely lauded, Spanish cinema is one of the best and most exciting national cinemas of the last decade, it has not been well supported by scholarly or journalistic writing on the subject. Certainly, the writing on Almodóvar is voluminous, but much as I admire his work, the work of one director, even one of the greatest, is not equivalent to one of the most vibrant and generative national cinemas in one of its most significant historical epochs, i.e., the Spanish Cinema of the post-Franco period 1975 to the present. It is in this context that Chris Perriam's *Stars and Masculinities in Spanish Cinema*, even were it is not half as good as it luckily is, will be seen as an essential work.

Perriam's project is clear from the Preface: 'What I intend is a contribution to Star Studies and Spanish Cultural and Flim Studies based on theorized close readings which link the production of character and personality on-and off-screen to the social and psychic construction of masculinities.' In other words, he is looking at male stars and how the types of men they embody and signify are constructed both by their films and by their press coverage. The book is divided into chapters each devoted to a particular star, excellent choices all, that follows a loose chronological order: Imanol Arias (Spain's Sweetheart of the 80s), pre-Hollywood Antonio Banderas (the confused and complex rebel of the 'new' Spain), Carmelo Gomez (the solid and sensitive leading man), Javier Bardem (the national star of 1990s Spanish cinema), Jordi Mollà (the current cinematic embodiment of Spanish masculinity in crisis) and Jorge Sanz (the child star of the 80s turned 90s farceur and clown). The last chapter is called 'A Newer Generation' and examines the personas of the most recent generation of male Spanish stars: Eduardo Noriega (*Abre los ojos/ Open Your Eyes*, 1997), Fele Martínez (*Los amantes del círculo polar/ Lovers of the Arctic Circle*, 1998), Liberto Rabal (*Carné tremula/ Live Flesh*, 1997), and Juan Diego Botto (*Historias del Kronen/ Stories of Kronen*, 1994).

Perriam is sensitive to issues of chronology, representation and the constant interplay between press coverage of the stars' roles in movies and the coverage of their personal lives. As such, as one reads, one feels one gets a good sense not only of each star's persona and the type of masculinity that it represents but also of how these change over time, a considerable achievement for which Perriam deserves great credit: unlike most academics, he has not only trawled

through the scholarly literature but he has also sifted through the archives of the popular press, not only movie magazines but lifestyle ones such as Hello. We thus not only get a context for the construction of star personas but also for their reception. We see how Arias' long relationship to actress and broadcaster Pastora Vega and their family life has influenced how he is cast and the reception of his roles; how the now mythic story of how Banderas arrived alone and with little money to Madrid is made use of in films like *Atame!/ Tie Me Up!Tie Me Down!* (1990); how Bardem is understood in the light of the film dynasty from which he comes (brother and sister are established actors, mother Pilar is famous character actress and great uncle Juan Antonio is one of the legendary directors of Spanish Cinema), etc.

Part of the pleasure of reading *Stars and Masculinities in Spanish Cinema* is that along with the rigorous readings of the films and the considered analysis of the star personas, it is also full of delightful plain old-fashioned information. We get to see all the films the stars were in, how they were billed, how much the films grossed in Spain. It's generous of Perriam, food for a scholar and heaven for a fan. With this information Perriam, with laudable integrity, provides all the tools necessary for the reader to argue with his thesis. And it is indeed in this way that one of the flaws in the book's main argument becomes apparent; for in looking at the detailed filmographies at the end of each chapter one begins to wonder if these

OXFORD

STARS AND MASCULINITIES IN SPANISH CINEMA

Chris Perriam

OXFORD STUDIES IN MODERN EUROPEAN CULTURE

Perriam does account for this in his introduction as he writes: 'the number of active performers in demand by the industry, their filmographies, their quickly consolidated careers, and the volume of printed and electronically mediatized coverage of their lives and roles, all argue if not for a Spanish star 'system' exactly, then certainly for a strong and specifically determined supporting matrix of image production, deals, outlets, tailored scripts, and simple star vehicles.'

Stars in the traditional sense or not, what Perriam proves beyond a doubt is that the leading actors of the past quarter century of Spanish cinema epitomise changing ideals of masculinity, that their

famous actors are stars at all. Certainly they have personas, but so do famous supporting actors (think, in Classic Hollywood cinema, of Eve Arden or Walter Brennan). Can actors who have supporting parts in one film, leading roles in another, who then go back to supporting roles and whose films are not consistently successful (e.g. Mollà and Sanz) be stars? Sometimes the book actually gives the impression that the only star of Spanish Cinema in the traditional sense is Bardem. Nonetheless developing star personas actually embody struggles around definitions of what it is to be a man in Spain, and that these struggles in turn represent a move into new and modern definitions of Spanish national identity. This is a thoughtful, admirably researched work sure to satisfy both scholars and fans and a great contribution to our knowledge of Spanish Cinema.

José Arroyo

The Conversations: Walter Murch and the Art of Editing Film
Michael Ondaatje
£25.00, 0747557748, Bloomsbury

Even before I opened this book, I had gone back to Ondaatje's early poetry: the visual sense that is so vivid in *The Collected Works of Billy The Kid*, the way the disparate elements, poetry and prose, combine, even the sense of sound:

> Sound up. Loud and vibrating in the room. My ears picking up all the burning hum of flies letting go across the room. The mattress under Pete Maxwell shifting its straw, each blade loud in its clear flick against another.

So I wasn't surprised, while preparing to interview Walter Murch, before this book was published, to read Ondaatje state that film editing was the stage of film 'closest to the art of writing'.

One of the things which the conversations between Ondaatje and Murch make clear is that we have a hard time finding the interface between art and craft. Ondaatje talks of writing in the dark, and then discovering in his editing process what it was he wrote; Murch describes the same process from the opposite side, putting together pictures and sound to discover what it was that was filmed. In both cases, the result may be very different from what was intended.

If you thought a discussion between a writer (who has made the occasional film) and the editor who worked on an adaptation of that writer's novel, *The English Patient* (1996) (and has written a

brilliant book of his own, *In The Blink Of An Eye*, on film editing) would be technical, rest assured it is anything but. Sitting up late at night, drinking coffee and brandy, reading Murch and Ondaatje exchanging ideas, making intuitive leaps, sharing their polyglot erudition, made me feel like a mute sitting at the next table in a Left Bank café. Fascinating but frustrating. The odd thing is, it is Murch who delivers the punchlines; Ondaatje is perhaps too much the writer to slip into the mode of performance which Murch has perhaps learned from a lifetime of working alone but in a team, surrounded by extravagant personalities.

More important, Murch is a man who makes connections, that is what he does, and that he what he sees. This is, I believe, what fascinated Ondaatje, and why he acts as the world's most erudite straightman to keep these conversations going, to examine everything from Murch's translations of Curzio Malaparte, to his father the painter,

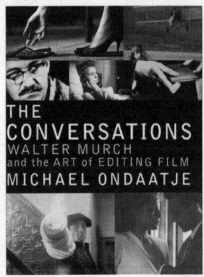

to the filming style of Fred Zinnemann. Of course, everything is there about those great films too: *The Godfather* (1972), *The Conversation* (1974), *Apocalypse Now* (1979), *American Graffiti* (1973) – the ones Murch worked on, and so many more.

Luckily for me, I have been assigned, at various times, to interview both these men. But neither experience, face to face, matched the rewards of this book. It's something to treasure for students of film, it's even more for those who care about the origins of art.

Michael Carlson

WALTER MURCH
THE SOUND OF SOUND

In an exclusive interview for *Kamera*, Michael Carlson interviews sound designer and editor Walter Murch, the subject of *The Conversations*, about Coppola, Welles and restoring 100-years old film.

*A*pocalypse Now begins with sound. The whirring chop-chop-chop of helicopter rotor-blades fades into the music of The Doors' 'The End', then rises again as the blades dissolve into the ceiling fan, under which Martin Sheen's Captain Willard lies grappling with inner demons. It is one of cinema's most powerful openings, a perfect melding of sound edits and visual edits.

Walter Murch won an Oscar as sound designer of *Apocalypse Now* (and was nominated for a second statuette as co-film editor). He won Oscars in the two categories for *The English Patient*, repeating a double he'd won from BAFTA for *The Conversation*. When we spoke in

The Conversation

London, I had recently watched another of his restoration projects, Orson Welles' *Touch Of Evil* (1958) and remarked how much that film was reflected in bits of *American Graffiti* and *The Conversation*.

MURCH: Yes, that was one of the things which drew me to the restoration project. The unravelling of that film is based on the spatial component of sound. I came to film sound because I developed a fascination with tape recorders in my teens, and I found I could funnel my interest in sound to film...the sonic landscape was undernourished—I wanted to bring in qualities of space.

In *Touch Of Evil* Quinlin is killed by a tape recorder...he hears the echo of what he's saying and understands immediately he's being recorded. Everything falls apart for him then, the entire film hangs on those sounds.

In The Making Of Citizen Kane, *Robert Carringer points out how much money Welles spent more than double the original budget on sound mixing and dubbing, and how much he used the techniques he'd learned in radio...*

Sound creates a deeper space you move through, you can see deeper into the image as a result. Hearing is the first of our senses to be turned on, some 4 _ months after conception. At birth it withdraws somewhat into the shadows.

In films, the mind projects sound back on the original object...for example, in *Apocalypse Now* sound associates the audience with Willard, the sound of his mind, and that's what involves you. He's a vehicle, through which you look at war and listen to it—like the subjective things in the sequence at the bridge: the sounds of conflict are replaced by the sound of construction, then that all goes away into absolute silence when Roach kills the sniper by using echo vibration.

I remember Ennio Morricone saying once that the human ear can only listen to two things at once.

In any one conceptual level, actually, it's two and a half. You can concentrate on two, with a half-layer is either exiting or entering, but three fully articulated layers is overwhelming, because they occupy different parts of the conceptual spectrum.

Can new technology impact that?

Well, with digital there's a great deal of immediacy...analogue has its virtues but its a technology at the end of its development, like the internal combustion engine. Normally you have encoded sound, which is speech, and embodied sound, like music, but digital is ALL encoded sound... Every stage has its adherents, but its like an architectural motif—painting frescos as opposed to pigment: you had a level of preparation which made it relatively inflexible, you had to prepare the surface of plasters and know how much you were going to paint, and by the end of the day reach into areas that may crack—but with pigment it's different.

Is the younger audience more attuned to the intricacies of sound design?

The biggest influence now is commercials on TV, where the rules are different. In fact, they're indifferent to the rules and what works is what we become conditioned to...

It's true visually as well.

There's no question that since 1950 the number of cuts per minute in feature films has accelerated, the theory is to pack as much in as you can to attract the eye, so you're as aggressive as possible with the image for no reason other than to catch the eye's attention...again that's commercials, or music videos, which are basically commercials for songs

Music videos brings me back to the link with Touch Of Evil, *the use of ambient sound to create a music track which you did on* American Graffiti...

The studio was Universal, as it had been with *Touch Of Evil*, and again they were completely resistant to the idea of a soundtrack album, completely, because what George (Lucas) and I wanted to do was commercially and artistically relatively innovative.

How important were your relationships with Lucas, or Francis Ford Coppola?

We were all very good friends. In fact, I met George at USC film school and met Francis through George, who Francis had hired to make a documentary about the filming of *The Rain People* (1969). In Hollywood everything was still compartmentalised, whereas in film school you did a lot of multi-tasking, so when Zoetrope was started in San

Francisco the Hollywood rules didn't apply. In Hollywood, for example, I wouldn't have been able to do both sound and editing on *The Conversation*.

Which is the other link with Touch Of Evil, *in the sense that* The Conversation *is a movie about tape recorders.*

I had lots of control on that film, because Francis was off shooting *The Godfather Part 2* (1974), and he just handed me the footage and said 'go do it' and I think because it was a film about a soundman he trusted me. I had the luxury of time because Paramount had absolutely no interest in the film—for them it was purely a ticket to *Godfather 2*. I worked on it for 14 months, but the problem was Francis had stopped shooting with two

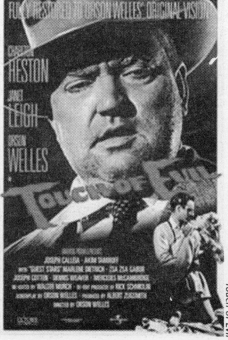

touch of evil

weeks to go, basically he'd run out of time and money, so there was about 20 minutes of script missing. We had to do one additional shot, of a hand pulling a tape off a reel, and it fit.

It was Coppolla who wanted what became 5.1 sound for Apocalypse Now?

Yes, and I'd only worked in mono, but Francis wanted quad sound, and he wanted sub-sonic sound, explosions that would hit you in the gut as well as the ears. Just before I joined *Apocalpyse*, I'd worked on *Julia* (1977) with Bill Rowe at Emi who'd done *Tommy* (1975) in quad. This led me to the 5.1 format: five channels, three behind the speaker, one back left, one back right, and one for low frequency information, and it became standard.

Apocalypse Now Redux *is a very different film, less episodic and more flowing. After Robert Duvall's famous paean to napalm, Willard (Martin Sheen) and his boat crew now steal Colonel Kilgore's surfboard. Willard becomes more human, but Kilgore (Duvall) becomes a less daunting psychopath, more of a buffoon.*

Kilgore tipped the balance of the film toward him, away from Kurtz. The new scenes balance things in a structural sense. The original idea came from our French distributor, who saw the documentary scenes of the French plantation and wondered if they still existed. Then Francis saw the film on TV here in London and said it felt ordinary to him. He felt it was time to go back to the original script. I was working on *The English Patient* at the time, and the idea of revisiting two years of work and two million feet of film made me nervous. But having done the recut of *Touch Of Evil* also emboldened me.

The French scenes provide a sort of mythic quality. It ends with that beautiful dissolve from a woman behind mosquito netting to fog on the river which suggests it's all a dream.

That was part of the intention. It becomes like Bunuel, a literally endless dinner conversation. You come out of the dream and arrive at Kurtz's nightmare.

Michael Ondaatje watched you work on the film of his novel and concluded editing was 'the stage of film closest to the art of writing...'

It was a technical challenge. It's extremely complex, with more time transitions than any film made until then. Sound can make those transitions, like the sound of a whistle Hanna (Juliette Binoche) is throwing while playing hopscotch blends into Arab music in Almasy's (Ralph Fiennes') head, and makes the jump in space and time. But the story also attracted me from the human point of view; how you take someone who is objectively evil, and allow the audience to sympathise with him.

You've done another restoration – of Thomas Edison.

It's a 17 second clip shot around 1894 of William Dickson playing violin, while two lab assistants dance, and on the left hand side of the picture is a big cone, which must've been attached to a recording cylinder. The cylinder had been thought lost until the Library of Congress found it, broken, and sent it to the Rogers and Hammerstein Archive who fixed and transcribed it. But the attempts to synch it failed because Edison shot at 40 frames per second and no one knew the speed of the cylinder. Rick Schmidlin, who'd got me involved with Touch Of Evil, sent it to me, I digitized it and crunched the image down to 24 frames per second, and spent the morning watching the fingering, which was familiar to me because my father played violin. Just as I was about to give up I found two good synch points, at beginning and end, and calculated what was in the middle mathematically. It was the first time it had been in synch in 106 years, if ever. There's also some more audio there, perhaps Edison himself, just ordinary 19th century conversation...

Interview by Michael Carlson

A City of Sadness
Berenice Reynaud
£8.99 ISBN 0851709303, BFI Publishing

Hou Hsiao-hsien's *City of Sadness* (1989) was the first Taiwanese film to touch on the events of 28 February 1949, when thousands of islanders were massacred in a demonstration against the increasing oppression of the government. Winning the Golden Lion at Venice and proving a success in Taiwan, the film is now seen as one of the cornerstones of the New Taiwanese Cinema that began in the early 1980s, not to mention world cinema in general. It is also the film that caught its director in a state of transformation; developing his earlier, looser style of film-making, into something more rigidly formal.

Berenice Reynaud's monograph is, for such a small book, surprisingly full of information about the film, Hou Hsiao-hsien's body of work, the movement he became associated with and Taiwanese history over the last century. The presence of such a wealth of information is mostly due to the way the author has structured the book. Most chapters open with a studied textual analysis of a certain scene or section of the film, whose main themes or elements are then developed to offer further insight.

After a brief overview of Hou's early life and the events that took place while the film was being made (the student demonstrations and ensuing violence in Tiananmen Square were happening as he edited his film, giving its themes an added resonance), chapter one presents a detailed analysis of the opening scene. With its

juxtaposition of the personal and political, Reynaud launches into a discussion of Taiwan's political history and how, out of the economic boom of the 1970s and a resulting relaxation in state censorship, the New Taiwanese Cinema grew in stature and influence. Likewise, chapter two uses a scene featuring the central characters to explore Hou's use of actors and his relationship with writers, discussing how the film was able to include details of the 28 February incident.

Reynaud also analyses the use of sound in the film (it was the first Taiwanese film to be shot with its soundtrack in synch) and develops her ideas to explore the way female characters are portrayed within Hou's films; their silence often proving louder than their words. Likewise, space is explored in the fourth chapter, drawing clear parallels with Ozu (although Hou only encountered the Japanese director's films after he had made eight of his own). Wong Kar-wai also offers an interesting comparison – certainly a major influence over Hou's recent, disappointing, *Millennium Mambo* (2001).

Reynaud's book is the first BFI Modern Classic to look at a South East Asian film and though the scope of her study is impressive, her writing style is not. It is a pity that the book lacks the enthusiasm the author must have had to produce so meticulous a study. The overriding remit of the BFI Classics and Modern Classics series should be to imbue the reader with a desire to seek out the film again. *A City of Sadness* offered interesting facts about the film's genesis and creative influences, but falls short of encapsulating the spirit of a film whose richness only shines through with repeated viewings.

Ian Haydn Smith

Soundscape: The School Of Sound Lectures 1998-2001

Edited by Larry Sider, Diane Freeman, and Jerry Sider
£15.99, 1903364590, Wallflower Press

There's an interesting dynamic to this collection of lectures, which opens with Mike Figgis' lament about the way films tend to be scored, as a final part of the industrial process, but which basically frames much of the rest of the discussion which follows as aberrational. Not because Figgis doesn't know what he is talking about, but because, as Walter Murch has said elsewhere, power on a film tends to flow to whoever controls a bottleneck of some kind. Once upon a time, in the early days of sound, the sound engineers had such power, but it was not to be long lived.

As Murch points out in his lecture, part

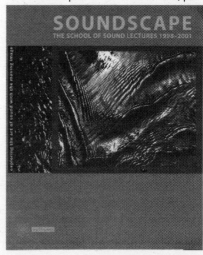

of which deals with his restoration of Welles' *Touch Of Evil*, Universal asked Henry Mancini to compose credits music, and when the credits were added over the opening sequence, so was the music. As Figgis might have said, so far so bad. But Welles' intent had been for the scene to flow with its ambient sound, the music coming from the radios of passing cars, out of bar doorways, or the open windows of tenement flats. This was what Murch restored, but the reason Welles lost it in the first place was because he had no way to bottleneck the process.

Laura Mulvey refers to the same period, making an essential point that the advent of sound coincided with the time of the Great Depression. Silent films were by definition international: they could be adapted to each market simply by translating the intertitles. When sound came, not only was Hollywood better able to adapt their production, they were equally able to take advantage of the weakened European market, fragmented by linguistic division. Mulvey is very good on the change in types of actors who became big in Hollywood – though it is embarrassing for a book about sound to mis-transcribe her reference to John Gilbert co-starring with Greta Garbo in *Flesh And The Devil* (1926) as John Garfield.

The lectures will take you as far as you care to listen: Manfred Eicher speaks about recording his European chamber jazz for his ECM record label: some of ECM strikes me as the musical equivalent of Bergman films, but much of it is as challenging as the *nouvelle vague*. There's even a long and somewhat tedious piece on sound in poetry by TV's Tom Paulin, which reminds me of the lectures about onomatopoeia one's high school teachers used to try to deliver over the onomatopoeic sound of boredom. James Leahy integrates poetry and film far better in a context which has space for both Keats and Howard Hawks. Shoma Chatterji reminds us of the cultural assumptions we bring to our perception of what sounds people and things make. And Carter Burwell brings the debate full circle, in his account of composing for the Coen Brothers. Not that he has a bottleneck in his hands; he's no Robert Johnson, but as he takes you through the Coens' oeuvre you recall that Robert Johnson features in *O Brother Where Art Thou?* (2000), a film that is about the way music becomes myth in America. There is literally something here for everyone. To hear.

Michael Carlson

Writers at the Movies
Edited by Jim Shepard
£11.95, 0714530743, Marion Boyars

Lurking behind Shepard's project I detect a tired British assumption that film is really a branch of literature. When I read that "fiction writers and poets are in some ways the ideal respondents to films", I become a very territorial film writer. After all, artists and photographers could also be regarded as the ideal respondents to films. Any background conceals as much as it reveals, of course. The emphasis on narrative and language here, a failure to see films by film historical lights, a reluctance to tackle the phantasm of a film flickering through our lives, keeps many of these accounts dead on the page. Mainstream film journalism may be paltry in places, but a fully-fledged film literature has gained all the contours of an original discipline.

The book's initial conceit seems to be its governing logic, meaning the result goes off in myriad directions. Poet Richard Howard loves the concert of images, sound, cutting and narrative phrasing in *A Man Escaped* (1956), but doesn't explore this experience beyond a page. I wonder from Edward Hirsch whether *Stevie* (1978) is still worth bothering with. The best pieces see the writer engage with the film as a *film*. Francine Prose on *The Godfather* (1972) is so good you wish she had a regular reviewing gig. Lorrie Moore really gets inside the hokum of *Titanic* (1998): 'Only hopeless romantics need to be told yet again that love is an illusion...The rest of us may just occasionally like – even love – a little respite from what we know.' Following a paean to *Titanic*'s cumulatively apocalyptic suffering, she writes: 'This is what Hollywood movies, so humanely, have always been for.' Cute but true. Discussing 1955's *Night of the Hunter* and its peculiar journey from horror to poetry, Charles Baxter writes of the children: 'It's as if the film is singing a lullaby to them that they can't hear.' Julian Barnes' description of Valentine Tessier's Emma in the 1933 Renoir adaptation of *Madame Bovary* – 'part tie-me-to-the-track silent-screen exaggeration' – is nicely impressionistic, not what many a film hack would have written. His lucid account of what Isabelle Huppert did with Emma in 1991 recalls provincial traps that are so peculiar to Chabrol. But in regard to the 1949 Vincente Minnelli version, Barnes simplifies the extent to which the film responded as much to particular post war American attitudes and Hollywood aesthetics as to Flaubert's novel. Salman Rushdie acknowledges that *The Wizard of Oz* (1939) may have been slow at the box office because it appeared two weeks before the outbreak of World War II. Why does he then not acknowledge that its 'Home vs. Away' textual schema resonates with isolationist American misgivings about involvement in forthcoming events? Again the failure to see films as breathing historical organisms.

Conversely, Philip Lopate writes

60

exuberantly about Godard's *Breathless* (1959) capturing the film's variegated manifesto status: genre revision, historical document, '60s advert, realist poem. Good film writing has this magpie energy. It is a pity that few writers or film critics understand this.

Richard Armstrong

Teach Yourself Screenwriting
Ray Frensham
£8.99, 0340859717, Teach Yourself Books

I once tried learning a language using one of these books, but always worried because I couldn't be sure I was giving the sounds their proper character. Screenwriting presents a similar problem. Although Ray Frensham can lay out the templates into which you can fit your writing, you can never be sure if the writing itself has the proper resonance.

The screenwriting business has transcended the art or craft itself. I remember an *Esquire* magazine cover with a chimp sitting at a typewriter, mug full of pencils at his side, cigarette in his mouth, captioned 'Is There Anyone In Los Angeles Who ISN'T Writing A Screenplay?' Today they'd need to include, at the very least, New York, London, and, if one happens to know a commissioning editor at BBC or Channel 4, most of the home counties. This has created a burgeoning market for men who make comfortable livings 'teaching' how to write screenplays, and for writers making even better livings writing movies about writing screenplays. And Ian Sinclair thinks Hollywood movies can't be self-referential enough to be art! Frensham, at least, advises newcomers to avoid writing in-jokes until they actually are IN the industry.

The best thing about this how-to manual is that it summarises Robert McKee well enough to save any chumps out there a lot of money. Practical advise is always useful if it sinks in, but sometimes its greatest value is to get the advisee to think. James Schamus once defined a screenplay as '120 pages of begging for money', and if you really must write one, at least your begging letter ought to be presented properly.

The dangerous thing about this, as with all guides to creative endeavour, is that they are wise only in retrospect. They tell you your screenplay must have a hot narrative hook in the first scene. It must have three acts, and so on. Well, yes and no. When you read the examples of narrative hooks listed, you realise many of them have been manhandled into the template retrospectively; they are seen to work now, because of the quality of what followed. *The Godfather* begins with a wedding, which establishes all the tensions and characters brilliantly, but where's the hook? It just shows that the main rule is there are no rules. If there were, the guys who write the books about the rules would be writing box office smashes instead. But because the industry is run by people who understand money, not fiction, templates help everyone rationalise, and you need to understand those rationalisations before you start writing your 120 pages.

Michael Carlson

The New Biographical Dictionary Of Film
David Thomson
£25.00, 03168559052 Little, Brown

I wish I could say that this latest edition of Thomson's Magnum Opus has taken a step forward. Earlier editions have been valuable starting points for me, and many others, in considering film-makers, not least because Thomson's succinct encapsulations have had a remarkable facility for finding the small details which illuminate larger truths about his subjects. It is precisely this sharp edge which appears to have been blunted in this re-titled 'new' edition.

Partly it is a problem of the times. There are so many new people whose work clamours for inclusion, and that is even before we delve far into the cult worlds of straight to video or DVD and made for TV movies; indeed, assembling a comprehensive filmography these days is a difficult task indeed, and it would be better for this volume were Thomson not even attempt to do so, especially as so many entries in this book are incomplete. It would also save space, for many entries are updated from past editions primarily by extending the filmography. It's no fun to read and, if not definitive, not very informative either.

The other problem of the times, of course, is that standards are so much lower, and so much seems so much less interesting. Is it just me (for I have certainly aged no more than Thomson since the last edition of the book appeared) or has he mellowed somewhat, is he more appreciative of the mainstream, has he elevated the literary and well-meaning to positions he would not have considered twenty-five years ago?

Or is it more that he has grown fonder of his own writing than the films he writes about? Thomson writes well, often facilely, which was wonderful when his insights were somewhat off-centre, caroming in from three cushions to just nudge the eight-ball into a side pocket. Now they seem more to be straight-ahead bangs into the corner, all English and no body.

Instead, he substitutes off-beat selections. According to my casual survey, in a book severely limited by space, the largest single entry, three full pages, belongs to Graham Greene. Among those accorded two full pages (or more) are Johnny Carson, Alan Bennett and Dennis Potter. Where an American TV comedian fits in with British novelists and playwrights is something that Thomson's essay, while perceptive, never explains.

Updating of existing entries results in some awkward copy errors, a reliance on sources who aren't always credited, but and there is the weird genuflecting before titles, 'Sir Charles Chaplin' for Charlie Chaplin, 'Lord David Puttnam' (*sic* – surely it should be David, Lord Puttnam of Thames TV or whatever) for David Puttnam. But despite its flaws, this book remains a monumentally entertaining compendium, more a compulsive read than an essential reference. If you need the latter, consult an earlier edition. In the meantime, the book's other title change, from 'A' dictionary to 'The' dictionary seems somewhat pretentious.

Michael Carlson

DVD Reviews

Every issue *Kamera* aims to provide readers with reviews of

the best or most noteworthy of recent DVD releases.

Our writers are informed, articulate and

passionate – if you want marks out of 5,

please look elsewhere.

Manhunter
(Michael Mann, 1986: Momentum)

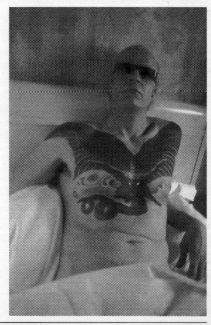

Despite its current reputation as one of
the most influential (and best) modern
policiers, Michael Mann's *Manhunter*
(1986) has had a very erratic distribution
history. An adaptation of Thomas Harris
second novel *Red Dragon*, the film was
released in the USA in August 1986 by
Dino De Laurentiis' DEG company, failing
to recoup its relatively modest $11 million
budget before disappearing from cinema
screens. This box office failure, coupled
with the financial collapse of DEG, meant
that it was not until February 1989 that
British audiences were able to judge the
film for themselves. This hiatus ran the

risk of already dating the film's ultra-modish styling, but a largely positive critical response was supported by the film's burgeoning cult following.

Inevitably, wider interest in the film was excited in the wake of *Silence of the Lambs* (1991) when long-term supporters of *Manhunter* keenly pointed out that Anthony Hopkins Oscar munching turn as Dr. Hannibal Lecter had been preceded by 5 years in a wholly different take on the literary world created by Harris. This led to comparisons between Brian Cox's and Hopkins' differing approaches to the role of the murderous doctor, with devotees of *Manhunter* bemoaning the fact that the latter's flamboyant theatrics had superseded the former's air of cool, understated menace.

Developing the stylistic approach that distinguished in his previous two features *Thief* (A.K.A. *Violent Streets*, 1981) and *The Keep* (1983) and his television series *Miami Vice*, Mann imbued the film with a dense combination of colour symbolism and visual abstraction while fully utilizing a range of modernist architectural spaces to convey the internal conflicts of its characters. Topped off by the director's penchant for narrative interludes underscored by a variety of classic and contemporary rock, *Manhunter*, despite its modern reputation as the film that introduced Lecter (or *Lecktor* as it is spelled here) to the cinema-going public, is a markedly idiosyncratic work. While the makers of the 2002 adaptation, *Red Dragon*, stressed their fidelity to Harris' text, Mann wilfully jettisoned several key narrative passages, foregrounding themes that have figured in much of his work.

Chief amongst these themes is the blurring of the line drawn between pursuers and the pursued. Through comprehension of, and empathy for, his monstrous quarry, Will Graham (William Petersen)'s psychological state undergoes its own gradual degeneration. This threatens not only his sanity but also serves to dismantle his familial security, the very target of the killer he is seeking to apprehend. Behaving in accordance with the lunar cycle, Francis Dollarhyde, *The Tooth Fairy* (Tom Noonan), is butchering entire families to satisfy his deluded fantasies. Alternately, Dollarhyde is shown to yearn for a chance at conventional romantic love but is doomed to succumb to his homicidal impulses. It is the range of contrasts drawn between Graham's and Dollarhyde's real and fantasy lives that provide the film's stylistic veneer with a genuine depth, negating common accusations that the film is an exercise in empty 1980s 'designer' style.

In light of the feminist debates that surrounded *Silence of the Lambs*, it is also striking now how *Manhunter* partly defines Dollarhyde's murderous rampage as an attempt to possess, dominate and destroy the family as it is conveyed through images of femininity. The killer chooses his victims through viewing the home movies of selected families, and central to these is the role of idealized mothers. At several points, Graham views the very same home movies and voices the killer's twisted desires ('God, she's beautiful!' exudes Graham in astonished recognition of Dollarhyde's erotic fixation), underlining just how dangerous he may have become to his own domestic stability. While this may run the risk of quasi-Freudian cliché, the film is wholly cognizant of the degrees of contrast in the act of 'seeing' and the role this plays in processes of domination and control. Refining the theoretical trope of a dominant masculine cinematic 'gaze', *Manhunter* attempts to draw distinctions between a wholly oppressive look and one that is more analytical and constructive. Indeed, it doesn't seem wholly accidental that during Graham's investigative epiphany, he concludes that for this particular killer, 'everything with you is *seeing*.'

Perhaps appropriately for a film so concerned with the obsessive allure of private image consumption, it has been repeat television screenings and home video that has helped to maintain the status of *Manhunter*. However, this is where the problems begin. Early British VHS releases replicated the film seen in cinemas and this remained the case with the first of three UK DVD incarnations in 1999 (on the BMG label, now a sought after collector's item). However, in 2001 Anchor Bay Entertainment released a double DVD edition in the USA that purported to contain both the theatrical version and a 'directors cut'. This release caused consternation among fans of the film, not only because the supposed 'theatrical version' inexplicably eliminated a couple of key dialogue passages (while reinstating other short sequences), but also because the so called 'director's cut' was a fuzzily transferred, badly framed rendition of a version that had first aired on the American Movie Channel station in 1988. The second UK release (on the Momentum label) replicated the 'theatrical version' seen on the American disc but did not contain the 'director's cut'.

This latest double disc edition, again by Momentum, still contains the same 'theatrical version' (as well as the theatrical trailer and featurettes, *Inside Manhunter* and *The Manhunter Look*) seen on their previous release, but also includes a superior (though far from perfect) transfer of the so called 'director's cut'. While the packaging assures the viewer/consumer that the film has been 'remastered', the film appears darker and many of the restored sequences have been taken from an obviously inferior source, resulting in a significant drop in picture quality whenever they appear. Mann reveals in his commentary track that this is because the original elements containing the reinstated footage had been lost after the collapse of DEG. In fact, Mann comments that this edition of the film should be considered the 'director's preferred version', the result of a re-think undergone after the initial theatrical release. However, there are still anomalies in this new edition that mean this is the *fourth* version of the film in circulation. The chief additions to the real theatrical version can be summarized thus:

After the title 'Manhunter' appears onscreen, the majority of the opening credits now play over the beginning of the sequence in which Jack Crawford (Dennis Farina) talks to Will Graham seated on a log on the beach. In the theatrical version, the credits all appeared before the main action commenced.

Prior to visiting Hannibal Lecktor, Graham calls his wife, Molly (Kim Greist), from his hotel room.

During the Atlanta police briefing, Graham addresses the officers and gives a few insights into the mind of the killer (some of the dialogue from this sequence ["his act fuels his fantasy"] appears in a different exchange after the briefing in the theatrical version).

During their face-to-face meeting, there is a brief extension to the dialogue in which Lecktor questions Graham's use of the word 'layman' to describe himself.

Before he examines the backyard of the Jacobi family, Graham has a brief exchange inside the house with a real estate agent (played by *Miami Vice* regular Michael Talbott).

After Graham is photographed with sleazy reporter Freddie Lounds (Stephen Lang), there is a brief exchange between Crawford and Graham in which Crawford reveals he has arranged for Molly to be flown in for the night.

Before the attempt to capture the killer in a midnight sting operation, there is a sequence in which Graham and Molly discuss their relationship in a hotel room before embracing against the Washington DC skyline.

After the final shootout at Dollarhyde's house, Graham visits the family that the killer had targeted as his next victims.

The main beneficiary of the additional sequences is Kim Greist, whose role as Molly is given much more screen time, providing greater insights into the troubles of her husband. However, while these additions provide viewers with a greater sense of the Grahams' tenuous domestic bond, the new director's cut is missing various passages and shots extant in other versions:

A slow reverse-zoom and dissolve away from

Graham and an ammunition expert prior to the attempted midnight sting.

Before visiting Lecktor, Graham talks briefly to Doctor Chilton (this sequence only appears in the Anchor Bay 'director's cut').

The most infamous excision from the Anchor Bay/Momentum 'theatrical version' has not been restored, suggesting Mann himself wasn't happy with it. In this sequence, just before Graham's decisive realisation, he delivers a monologue about the origins of the killer as an 'abused kid, a battered infant... somebody took a kid and manufactured a monster.' The rest of the missing sequence emphasises how Graham can both empathise and *sympathise* with killers while recognising the dire urgency to stop them – 'My heart bleeds for him as a kid... As an adult, somebody should blow the sick fuck out of his socks.'

The death throes of Dollarhyde are slightly less graphic, reduced from 5 shots to three.

As Graham and Reba embrace in long shot after the shootout, the dialogue exchange 'Who are you?' 'I'm Graham, I'm Will Graham' has been eliminated.

Just before the final sequence, a shot of Graham silhouetted on a boardwalk against the dawn skyline has been removed.

While Mann's somewhat sporadic commentary doesn't elaborate too much on the reasons for these changes, he provides some interesting insights regarding the issues and themes that attracted him to the project. Other anecdotal revelations include; the identity of the real life murderer upon whom he based his interpretation of Dollarhyde; the

reason he chose Iron Butterfly's 'In A Gadda Da Vida' as the musical accompaniment to the final shootout; the sequence that was inspired by a Rock Hudson/Doris Day phone conversation in *Pillow Talk* (!); and the reasons for the title change mid-shoot. Perhaps ironically, Mann does not provide information on an image that has never appeared in any version of the film but has graced the cover of every DVD release in the UK and USA - a topless Dollarhyde revealing a giant tattoo of a red dragon on his torso. Also Mann does not mention that a 1986 episode of *Miami Vice* ('Shadow in the Dark) was effectively a 50 minute digest version of *Manhunter*, an effective little companion piece to the film that has been little remarked upon.

If this is indeed Mann's preferred version then the presentation on this disc is another missed opportunity. The transfer itself is inferior to the accompanying 'theatrical version' (which remains the best *looking* edition of the film) and the use of inferior materials for the restored sequences is regrettable. If the original elements for the restored passages did indeed go missing after DEG's collapse, it is possible we will never see a truly definitive restoration of *Manhunter*. Unless Dino knows differently of course...

Neil Jackson

With acknowledgement to: Tim Lucas, 'Michael Mann's *Manhunter:* Spread Your Wings And Learn To Die'; Paul M Sammon, 'The Unseen Manhunter: The Slaying Of *Red Dragon*' in *Video Watchdog*, No. 13, Sept/October 1992.

Manga: The Collection
(Directors vary: Manga Entertainment)

Animation, particularly cell animation, is something many people still mistakenly assume is "strictly for kids". Not so in Japan. In Japan animation – *anime* – is a medium to be explored the same as any other, the result being a diverse range of titles covering every genre from teen romance to science fiction, and horror to comedy. Despite previous attempts, it was Katsuhiro Otomo's remarkable *Akira* (1988 - based on his own epic *manga*) that really brought *anime* kicking and screaming into the UK. It took audiences' breath away with its startling blend of cyberpunk aesthetics, apocalyptic vision and complex plotting combined with exhilarating set-pieces and occasionally graphic violence. Soon *anime/manga* in

the UK would become associated with certain types of film - those with high levels of violence and sex, the most notorious of which involved the demonic atrocities of *Urotsukidoji* (Hideki Takayama, 1989). However the range of *anime* extends far beyond this and can encompass such esoteric fare as *Ushio and Tora* (1992) and the truly insane *Urusei Yatsura* (TV series from 1981). Similarly the films of master animator Hayao Miyazaki surpass the detail of even the very best of Disney and are devoid of exploitative material, remaining utterly delightful and resolutely Japanese.

Anime is quite different to the Western perception of animation - plots can be intense, the subject matter confrontational or technologically in-depth and the animation techniques strikingly different. It is this latter factor that places *anime* in its own world - whip-blur backgrounds give a sense of dynamism, unusual angles are employed, and techniques such as faked slow-motion, fogging or digital processing go a long way to forming the overall aesthetic. At the forefront of the UK's mainstream *anime* onslaught is (the confusingly named) Manga Video. They are broadening the market away from the *otaku no video* (video geeks) with the introduction of a new series of DVDs. These are neatly packaged to sit comfortably alongside one another, are numbered in *kanji* along the spines (gotta catch 'em all) and priced low enough to encourage impulse purchasing for the curious. DVD is the ideal format for *anime* as it is capable of reproducing saturated colours and copes very well with compression. There is, however, one caveat when it comes to Manga's initial roll-out of The Collection: with the exception of *Amon Saga* there is no option to watch the films in their original language with subtitles. It's a real shame as one of DVDs' plus points is the facility to have multiple soundtracks/subtitles. So, how do they fare?

Amon Saga / Shunji Oga (1986)

Fantasy and revenge are the themes of this richly detailed and beautifully designed feature length *anime*. Emperor Valhiss is a power-crazed tyrant who commands his evil armies housed on the back of a giant city-sized tortoise. He holds green-haired Princess Lichia captive to obtain a map to the City of Gold from her father. Meanwhile our hero Amon seeks vengeance for his mother's death by enlisting in Valhiss' imperial army in order to infiltrate it, but he falls for the princess' charms. This is stirring fantasy with that old-meets-new feel that owes more than a nod to Miyazaki's *Laputa: Castle in the Sky* (1986). The animation is at times startling with the highlight being the huge tortoise lumbering to its next destination, swarming with dragons and flying machines. Good stuff.

Landlock / Tekeshi Waki (1996)

Many *anime* feature characters with huge eyes, normally giving them a *kawaii* (cute) appearance. *Landlock* is no exception but here Luda and Agahali each have differently coloured eyes, unusual ocular anomalies that could be the key to power over the God of Wind. Evil overlord Zanark wants that power to rule the world and thinks nothing of deception and slaughter to further his insidious goals. Luda meanwhile, who has trained to be the (unfortunately titled) Master of the Wind, seeks vengeance for the death of his father and ransacking of his village. Technology and magic sit side by side as interconnected god statues, flying machines and advanced weaponry mix with rural simplicity and low-tech mechanics. Visually *Landlock* excels with its large scale set pieces as well as low-key character based tension, all of which are superbly animated and exceptionally designed. A superior, easy to watch adventure romp.

Psychic Wars / Tetsuo Imazawa (1991)
When surgeon Ukyo removes a tumour from an aged woman he unsurprisingly doesn't expect the cancerous growth to mutate and attack people. Nor does he anticipate receiving enhanced psychic abilities when the woman dies, powers that enable him to fight towering green-blooded demons with weapons summoned by his thoughts alone. He has inherited the powers of the gods to fight a holy war thousands of years in the past to prevent the whole future history of Japan falling into the demons' hands. *Psychic Wars* is *anime* at its low budget best. The parade of visual ideas is seemingly endless – sepia toned sections, red-haired flying psychic vampire women, sinister nuns, moss covered shrines and lots of demon fighting. The inventiveness and careful use of backlighting more than compensate for the long static shots and the limited number of cells used.

Sword For Truth / Osamu Dezaki (1990)
Another unapologeticly lurid tale from the prolific Toei Studios. Princess Mayu has been kidnapped. The ransom: the Ginryu sword. The penalty for non-compliance? Well these are ruthless brigand ninjas, so she faces rape and death. Who can stop these nefarious ninja 'nappers? Enter Shuranosuke, beefy blade bloke hired by the Tokugawa Shogunate for just that purpose – oh, and for some diverting rumpy pumpy between bouts of ultraviolent swordplay. Honest, unabashed gratuitous exploitation that plays to the stalls.

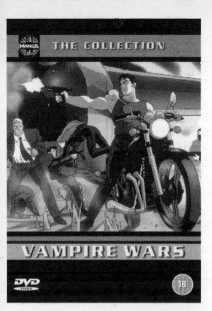

Vampire Wars / Kazuhisa Takenouchi (1991)

More vaguely suspect über-gore from Toei as Kuki, as extreme an anti-hero as you could imagine, is coerced into becoming a French secret agent by liberal application of electric shocks. To add to his troubles there's a group of vampires on the loose, carving a bloody swathe through anyone who gets in their way. *Vampire Wars* packs a lot into its slim running time with a ridiculous amount of bodies riddled with bullets or gouged by vampiric teeth and all sorts of plot twists. The nature of the vampires is strangely reminiscent of early Jean Rollin films - their origins more science fiction than folklore based. Sadly the budget limitations do take their toll in a couple of sequences and some of the dialogue is unintentionally hilarious, but overall the bizarre narrative thrust and graphic bloodletting go some way to compensate for this.

Red Hawk Weapon of Death / Sang Il Sum, Jung Yul Hwang (1995)

Anime is associated primarily with Japan but, rather like a number of US TV animations, a large number of productions farm their work out to Korea, which, as a result, has a huge animation industry of its own. *Red Hawk* is an example of this. The head honcho of the notorious Five Dragons group in the Camellia Blossoms gang is set to rule the land with an iron fist and some impressive chest expanding martial arts skills. But first he's after the blood of traitor Danlyong, who travels the country incognito, pausing occasionally to change into Red Hawk, champion of the oppressed. With a small band of friends Danlyong aims to confront the evil Lord. This is unabashed entertainment which liberally borrows from familiar *anime* territory (*Dragonball* is a notable example) and is not ashamed to revel in its Boys

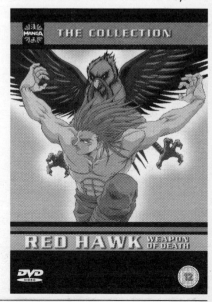

Own heroics. As the tale progresses Red Hawk's superior powers are revealed ("You've mastered levitation - damn you!" exclaims a baddie), but so are his increasingly camp enemies' bewildering arsenals of cunning gadgets and pseudo-mysticism. Harmless adventure for lovers of cartoons, martial arts and American wrestling.

Colin Odell and Michelle Le Blanc

Bande à part
(Jean-Luc Godard, 1964: BFI)

In the opening titles of *Bande à part* Jean-Luc Godard announces that he does not make films – he makes cinéma. Godard is telling us that he is not making something out of a physical piece of film but that he is making something that is part of the history of cinema. He is a critic, in the sense that he uses his cinema to comment upon the past and future of cinema.

For example, much of the opening sequence of *Bande à part* is shot from the back seat of a car, watching the backs of our heroes Arthur Rimbaud (not the poet) and Franz Kafka (not the author) as they talk about the money they are going to steal with Odile's help. It feels like the bank robbery in *Gun Crazy* (1949), but Godard subverts the tension by having his characters talk about lots of different things, things that are not relevant to the plot.

There are other references to cinema, including Charlie Chaplin (the dance of the bread loaves from *The Gold Rush* (1925) and *The Immigrant* (1917)), Lev Kuleshov (is the man on the Metro nice or vicious?), westerns and B-movies. But cinema is just one aspect of the artistic firmament that Godard enthuses about. The references to the poetry of T.S. Eliot ('everything that is new is automatically traditional') and Arthur Rimbaud (there are many quotes throughout), the books of Jack London, Edgar Allan Poe ('The Purloined Letter') and Raymond Queaneu, and the plays of William Shakespeare (*Romeo and Juliet*), mix with songs, newspapers and art (the principles run through the Louvre). There is a temptation to view the film as a sort of game, where you try to find as many allusions and references as possible. In fact, this DVD from the BFI contains an A to Z full of such information so that you can check your score afterwards.

In a short but sweet interview on the DVD, cinematographer Raoul Coutard explains that Godard would turn up on set with bits and pieces of dialogue and action that he had written overnight. If they ran out of things to film, the cast and crew would simply wait around until Godard wrote something for them. The film had to be about 90 minutes in duration and it was running short, so Godard told the actors to read out murders from the newspaper to get the additional footage. This reliance on intuition and spontaneity shows in the final film, giving it a lightness of touch as it bounces between the two plots: the robbery and the love story.

Although *Bande à part* has a robbery, it is not very well planned and is amateurishly executed by the characters. The love story is of far more interest, as shy Odile (Anna Karina) is entranced by the powerful and dark Arthur (Claude Brasseur) whilst poetic Franz (Sami Frey) pines after her. Towards the end, when Odile and Franz are together, he says that two people can never form a complete whole, that they must remain apart. Godard illustrates this most succinctly in the famous sequence when the three characters are dancing The Madison in a café. As they dance, Godard replaces the music with his voice, explaining the motivation of each character and thus pointing out that even though dancing (and robbery) is a group activity, they are still separate people. Even the title of the film (*Bande à part* – literally 'a group apart from others' but also perhaps from each other) hints at this. This is an appropriate theme for a robbery where genre convention dictates that after the robbery the group will destroy each other. But, of course, Godard subverts the genre (and his own films, because separation/alienation/apartness is a recurring theme of his work) by having the lovers sail off to Brazil and live happily ever after... in Cinemascope and Technicolor.

The subversion extends to all aspects of the film. When Karina says that one minute of silence is an eternity, the characters stop speaking and all sound is turned off for a minute. And yes, it is a long time. We know that Godard is doing the subverting because he speaks to us 23 times over the course of the film. In one amusing voice over, he explains what has happened so far for those who have arrived late. There is no doubt that Godard is the author of the film, the puppeteer of his mannequins, in control of the images, sound and editing. Yes, perhaps Godard is right. Perhaps he is cinéma.

Ironically for a film that references so many other films and arts, *Bande à part* has become part of cinema history and is now referenced more often than it is seen. The joyful dance sequence has been 'appropriated' by Hal Hartley (in *Simple Men* (1992)) and then by Quentin Tarantino (in *Pulp Fiction* (1994)) but Godard's intention cannot be mimicked or reproduced. He is an original in the truest sense of the word, and now you can 'appropriate' the whole of *Bande à part* for yourself.

Paul Duncan

The Swordsman
(King Hu, 1990 – Acting Directors: Tsui Hark, Ching Sui Tung, Raymond Lee: Hong Kong Legends)

The stylistic debt that the Hong Kong martial arts film, particularly the *Wu Xia* or swordplay film, owes to King Hu is immense. His films are poetic, dynamic and filled with astonishing images. More than that he introduced respectability into the genre, and was nominated for the Palme d'Or at Cannes for his epic *A Touch of Zen* (1969). Acknowledging King Hu's place in Hong Kong cinema history, influential director/producer Tsui Hark brought the esteemed director out of retirement to helm *The Swordsman* - an ambitious attempt to revitalise a genre that had been in decline. However, due to a number of artistic differences Hu left the production and, despite retaining credit, the film was completed by a number of other directors.

The Swordsman follows the adventures of Wah School pupils Ling and his sidekick 'Kiddo', a female martial artist whose male disguise really shouldn't fool anyone. They are on the trail of the sacred scroll, stolen from the libraries of the Forbidden City, which purports to reveal martial arts secrets of immense power. This power must indeed be great, as a variety of clan leaders, including villains Zhor and Ngok, are vying for the scroll and already possess extraordinary prowess. Although adept with the sword, both Ling and 'Kiddo' have much to learn, both physically and spiritually.

This is an astonishing film, packed to the brim with exhilarating wire-work and incredible imagery. Those seeking any degree of realism would be advised to steer well clear, as this is a fantastical expressionist work unrestrained by any conventional notion of physics or human limitations. Live snakes emerge from sleeves as deadly weapons, stone altars are bisected by whips, bodies spiral skyward in flight and a single sword can fell an army. All this is filmed in a highly stylised manner, exquisitely shot, cutting from deep reds and magic hour landscapes to strong blue duo-tonal interiors. Despite the pathos and the liberal bloodletting, there is also a great deal of humour on show, normally centred on Kiddo vainly trying to disguise her femininity or bungling some stealthy errand. If that were not enough there is even time for a musical interlude which, far from being superfluous, is essential to the plot and, rather like Tsui Hark's *Once Upon A Time In China* (1991), provides an aural motif throughout the film. *The Swordsman* spawned two sequels that, remarkably, manage to expand the fantastical elements even further.

Colin Odell and Michelle Le Blanc

Mark of the Devil
(Michael Armstrong, 1969: Anchor Bay)

Films based upon real life atrocities have consistently proved to be a great way of appealing to the exploitation market and baiting the censor. The Inquisition (and other forms of religiously fuelled persecution) has provided an ideal excuse for film-makers to delight in the torture of innocents. There are of course several excellent examples of

intelligent, shocking film-making within this particular genre - from Benjamin Christensen's astonishing *Haxan* (1921) to Ken Russell's delirious *The Devils* (1971). One of the most financially successful was Michael Reeves' *Witchfinder General* (1968), an unremittingly bleak portrayal of England under the grip of Matthew Hopkins, a sadistic hypocrite played with icy horror by Vincent Price. Despite the film's earnest tone and despairingly gloomy outcome, its success spawned many a cash-in, of which *Mark of the Devil* is the most notorious. Indeed the film's lurid US campaign featured complimentary sick bags and the warning "likely to upset your stomach".

As the pious sounding baritone informs us, this is a tale 'taken from history' - a sombre earnestness that doesn't quite tally with the previous few minutes of *Sound of Music* landscapes, raped nuns, finger chopping and women being strung up and burned alive. But more is to come as Lord Cumberland, unimpressed with the current witchfinder, seeks to do a better job himself. Instead of heaving the 'witches' onto the next bundle of smouldering sticks, he prefers the hands-on approach of diabolical torture and pre-pyre rapings. We are in sleazy exploitation territory here, albeit filmed in the Hammer period style – all heaving bosomed wenches, yokels and stone castles of indeterminate age. Where Hammer gave us a cosy fairy-tale evil, Michael Armstrong's film looks to the cold despair of *Witchfinder General* but, despite being far more graphic, fails to reproduce the fetid air of futility that permeated Reeves' classic. Instead Armstrong peppers his film with torture – the notorious rack followed by a tongue ripping scene, strawberry-jam coloured floggings and a charming moment when an accused man is forced to sit on a seat of nails before having his feet branded.

Despite its salacious dialogue, the 'V for Violence' faux-rating and its fearsome reputation, *Mark of the Devil* seems a bit anaemic in this postmodern age, despite its parade of atrocities. This is at least partly down to the print used in this DVD transfer – the trailers and short feature accompanying the DVD include brief shots of a far more graphic and exploitative nature. It is the very *raison d'etre* of the exploitation film that it should be irresponsible and unacceptable. In its reissued form *Mark of the Devil* just isn't offensive or disreputable enough.

Colin Odell and Michelle Le Blanc

Big Wednesday
(John Milius, 1978: Warner Home Video)

A surfing devotee following his shoe father salesman's relocation of his family to California – he claims to have been on a board by the age of ten – John Milius' *Big Wednesday* is a personal and highly evocative hymn to both surfing and beach life in general that also offers a poignant 1962-1974 chronicle of friendships and lifestyles in transition.

Milius' third feature as director following the bravura, Warren Oates starrer *Dillinger* (1973) and the similarly confident *The Wind and the Lion* (1975), it's now popularly viewed as a seminal work and one of the most remarkable American films of the seventies. This contemporary view is an act of revisionism; upon its release critics bemoaned the film's loose narrative structure and melancholic mediation upon the American dream. Much worse, they detected a Nietzschean streak and labelled Milius a reactionary. Moreover, the film achieved strictly meagre box office returns, much to the chagrin of George Lucas who in a profit sharing scheme – offered at Lucas' suggestion – had exchanged points in his own *Star Wars* in return for a stake in *Big Wednesday*.

Both celebrating and questioning traditional values (with one of the best scenes comically depicting the extent to which the obscenely tanned, toned and healthy California youths will go to escape the Vietnam draft), *Big Wednesday* follows buddies Matt, Jack and Leroy as they search for the perfect 20-foot swell. Relative newcomers Jan-Michael Vincent

(never better), William Katt and Gary Busey (all too infrequently better) are perfectly cast as the somewhat narcissistic trio whose friendships slowly deteriorate as external forces, primarily Vietnam and the pressure to assume responsibility, exert their inexorable and suffocating hold. In terms of comparison pictures, only Bogdanovich's *The Last Picture Show* (1971) comes close to capturing the same feeling of change, longing and regret.

Co-written by Dennis Aaberg and Milius, who had already established an estimable track record as a writer for hire in Hollywood with a penchant for flawed masculinity (*Evel Knievel*, 1971, *Dirty Harry*, 1971 and the Indianapolis monologue from *Jaws*, 1975, are amongst his early credits), *Big Wednesday* is a technical *tour de force*. Beautifully rendered by Bruce Surtees, who subsequently went on to forge a fruitful cinematographic relationship with Clint

Eastwood with surfing sequences produced by Greg Mac Gillivray, the film's explicit consideration of the interaction and dichotomy between man and nature is redolent of Terrence Malick. On a more purely sensory level, the surfing sequences are thrillingly invigorating with the camera travelling both within and beneath the mighty fifteen-foot waves.

Though Milius' would frequently return to similar themes in his own, increasingly disappointing films and those he more satisfyingly penned for others – the surfing sequences in Coppola's Wagnerian *Apocalypse Now* (1979) belong to him – he would never better *Big Wednesday*, a fact he more or less acknowledges in the fascinating and insightful interview that appears amongst the extras on this new DVD. An edifying feature length commentary and the obligatory original trailer also appear. Though brisk at only twenty minutes, the interview is revealing of the director's favouring of proletarian heroes and his insistence that his lead performers, whose characters were all based on composites of real people drawn from Milius' surfing community, navigate the majority of their own surfing sequences. Presented here in a beautiful transfer, *Big Wednesday*'s mythic status is very much deserved.

Jason Wood

Badlands
(Terrence Malick, 1973: Warner Home Video)

In the short documentary featured on the new DVD release of *Badlands* (1973), actors and crew talk about their experiences of working on set. The shooting of that film was the yardstick by which I measure all other film experiences, admires Sissy Spacek; her husband Jack Fisk, the production designer acknowledges it as the first time he saw that film could be an art form ; of the director Terrence Malick, Martin Sheen declares, we knew that we were at the birth of a very special artist in cinema . The reclusive Malick himself does not feature in the documentary hence its title, *Absence of Malick*, although, as pointed out, he does appear in *Badlands*, not only once (which is relatively well-known) as the man who comes to the door of the rich man s house, but on another fleeting moment (which is less conspicuous) during the black and white sequences, dressed in a trench coat and trilby. Sheen, Spacek, Fisk and Billy Weber the editor, who is also interviewed, are clearly devoted fans, and it's easy to see why *Badlands* worked wonders for their careers. Fisk and Weber joined with him subsequently on *Days of Heaven* (1978) and *The Thin Red Line* (1998). Spacek and Sheen, both unknowns, received the kind of critical attention that actors dream of, and deservedly so; their performances are flawless. Sheen, aged 31, plays the 19-year-old Kit Carruthers (a character based on 1958 real-life serial killer Charlie Starkweather) with an alarming mix of youthful verve and heedless action. Spacek, as his 13-year-old girlfriend Holly, is a blank canvass of a girl on the brink of self-discovery, feeling her way around romance and responsibility after the death of her father (at Kit's hand). Lovers on the run, they drive across the wide-open

MARTIN SHEEN SISSY SPACEK

Badlands

From Terrence Malick, the director of
Days of Heaven and The Thin Red Line.

18

badlands of Montana, making their temporary home in a tree house in the woods, living out a wilderness fantasy that cannot sustain itself, forced inexorably on the road time and time again. Malick's predilection for spontaneously moving shots that had already been set up to film elsewhere, while trying for his crew, was worth the angst it must have caused. Every single scene feels weighted, significant, portentous even, a tone which is heightened through the masterful integration of the music of Eric Satie, James Taylor and Carl Orff. On the face of it a small film, about apparently motiveless, almost arbitrary, killing, Malick deftly moves between grandiose backdrops and minute details. Such precision, combined with sure acting style and stunning cinematography, results in a film that is at once remote and intense. Aside from the documentary, there are no other special features on the DVD. But as one of the best youth/road/killers-on-the-run/rites of passage movies ever made it is well worth having for the collection, not least because the music, sadly, isn't available on CD.

Hannah Patterson

The Nature of National Cinema

What do we mean by 'National Cinema'? Although shot and largely cast in the UK and celebrated as 'British' films by the British (or, more precisely, English) media, such films as *Shakespeare in Love* and *The Full Monty* were wholly financed by US companies who retained all the profits. Are they, therefore, any more 'British' than, for example, *American Beauty* – shot and financed in the US, but directed by an Englishman (Sam Mendes)?

In the first of Kamera's 'Megaphone' columns – designed to air important issues in cinema today – **Andrew M. Butler** explores the quirks and contradictions inherent in 'national cinema' as part of a globalised industry.

There's an understandable tendency to think of Hollywood when thinking of film –Tinseltown is clearly the centre of the film-making world in terms of world dominance, and surely more money is spent there than anywhere else. At cinemas in Britain most films shown are American. Partially this is sheer numbers – more films are made in the US than in Britain – but as well as production, it is also to do with the economics of distribution – who distributes the films, and who shows them.

In a Hollywood film the language used is likely to be English, the camerawork, dubbing and other production values will at least be adequate, and it's unlikely to really challenge the viewer or make them suffer for their art. Indeed art, aesthetics, might not even come into it – we are being sold a fairground ride with someone pretty to look at or identify with for ninety minutes or more. But how far is this true of the films made in countries all over the world?

With much of this output there is a language barrier which can be partially crossed by using subtitles. Sometimes the production values are not what we are used to in Hollywood product. And films can depict cultural practices and share cultural assumptions that we are not familiar with.

Rather than reject this material sight unseen, any difficulties should be embraced; anyone who limits themselves to Hollywood products is literally missing out on a world of wonders. The worldwide success of *Crouching Tiger, Hidden Dragon* (2000) obscures scores of (frankly much more interesting) Hong Kong films which don't necessarily have to involve Jackie Chan. India – best known for Bollywood films – actually produces more films than Hollywood, although comparatively few make it to the west. Films are made throughout Europe, and Latin America is fertile ground for investigation. Then there is English language film, from Britain, obviously, but also from Ireland, Canada (which also has Francophone films), New Zealand and, most importantly for this article, Australia.

National Cinema is, at its simplest, the cinematic product of a given country. Of course, it isn't *quite* that simple, but for now let's maintain the illusion. Under this definition, Hollywood is itself a national cinema, the nation in this case being the United States of America. In film studies, National Cinema should be the label given to the study of films from a given country which pays particular attention to the production context (funding bodies and production facilities) and distribution networks that allow those films to be exhibited.

Additionally, these films are studied for the way they display, critique or create a sense of national identity. National identity is the set of characteristics held in common by citizens of a particular country, or those characteristics which are recognised as such by the community. Identity is created or recognised through language, stories, ideologies and myths, and can be used by the dominant members of a national power structure to justify their own position as rightful rulers. These characteristics may be thought of as constituting a stereotype, or more charitably an archetype; at the same time they are not just imposed by the state. They can be created, recognised or challenged by the individual: to depict a national stereotype may be as much to hold it up to ridicule as engage in an act of patriotism.

Just as the national characteristics vary between countries, so do the contexts of production. Because the creation of a national character is in the interests of state, either for ruling its citizens at home or exporting a product (material or ideological or both) abroad, in many countries the government has input into the film industry. This might be tax breaks for investment, quotas of how much domestic product must be shown at cinemas or on television, or actual investment or subsidy via Arts Councils and Film Commissions. When money is invested, it comes with strings attached, such as the choice of lead actor (usually someone from the paying country), technicians or facilities. The money might be given to a director and producer who have come together for a particular project in isolation, or it might be within some kind of studio context.

Once the film is completed, it needs to be shown – but there is no guarantee that it will be. In Britain many more films are made than exhibited theatrically and so hundreds of films languish in distribution limbo. There is the film festival circuit An audience or jury prize is one way to aid gaining distribution contracts but often the event is a space for launching a deal rather than closing one. In any case, the festival is not sufficient in itself to make a film commercially successful, though the publicity gained is invaluable.

Because there is no guarantee of international success, the producer has to aim to make most money back in the domestic market.

The actuality doesn't always match the theory. Mike Hodges' film *Croupier* (1997), featuring Clive Owen as a wannabe writer who gains work at a casino, sank without trace on first release in Britain; as one of the few people who saw it (at a festival) I think this was unfair. Although it was no *Get Carter* (1971) or *Flash Gordon* (1980), it deserved an airing. It only got a (slightly) wider distribution in Britain after it became an unexpected hit in America. In addition US made films such as *Memento* (2000) and *O Brother, Where Art Thou?* (2000) were first exhibited in Britain before gaining an American release.

Another source of income is television and video cassette/DVD rights. The French cable television company Canal Plus is a frequent investor both in French films and films from across Europe, as well as in some of the more independently-minded American directors. Within Britain the establishment of Channel 4 as a minority interests channel led to the creation of a television broadcaster which commissioned films with a guarantee of television showings. The BBC has also ventured from time to time into funding feature films, although initially these films could only be shown cinematically outside of Britain, in part because of

rights agreements negotiated with acting and technicians' unions, in part to maximise viewers for the television premiere.

Directors of less commercial films may find themselves having to attract funding from several such bodies, from several countries, each with their own demands. A Peter Greenaway movie such as *The Baby Of Mâcon* (1993) has to look for money from The Netherlands, France and Germany along with British funds. Is it a British film because the director hails from these shores? Then there's an Australian film like *The Piano* (1993), which was directed by Jane Campion, a New Zealander, is set in Scotland and New Zealand and stars two Americans – Harvey Keitel and Holly Hunter.

(I said it would get more complicated.)

More examples: the Canadian director Atom Egoyan's *Felicia's Journey* (1999), shot in Birmingham UK, is a US/Canadian co-production, *Dark City* (1997) and *The Matrix* (1999) are both Hollywood films shot in Australian-based studios owned by American studios – except of course that it depends what you mean by 'American'. Twentieth-Century Fox is part of Australian Rupert Murdoch's News Corp. empire, and ownership of other studios can be traced to Japanese and other Far Eastern financiers. *Dark City* and *The Matrix* were presumably made with an eye on the American market, as was *Moulin Rouge* (2001 – set in France, shot in Australia, directed by an Australian, starring an Australian who's made most of her recent films in Hollywood, alongside several British actors and the odd American). Is this an Australian export? Or American exploitation of Australian resources?

National Cinemas

As an article of this size cannot describe all the intricacies of the various national cinemas, I'm going to concentrate on the Australian situation, but first a brief word on some others.

France has been through a number of periods of film-making, with perhaps the most significant period being the 1960s and the *Nouvelle Vague* (or New Wave). Many of the critics who had been working on the film journal *Cahiers du cinéma*, from which the *auteur* theory had emerged, began to make their own films, most notably Jean-Luc Godard, François Truffaut and Claude Chabrol. This generation of film-makers was attempting to make a distinct break from the quality cinema of the previous generation and produced non-linear, morally ambiguous and stylistically complex movies. Shooting on the streets of Paris or in each others' apartments, and often casting friends and girlfriends in rôles, Godard brought a new sense of verisimilitude to film. As the decade progressed, the films became more political. The key film is probably *A Bout De Souffle* (1959) directed by Godard.

Spain's film history is dominated by its political landscape – thanks to the dictatorial rule of General Francisco Franco from 1936 to 1975 there were strict limitations on what kinds of films were allowed to be made, and unlike many film-producing countries there were no film schools to train directors. In the years after Franco's death rules relaxed so much in Spain that it is now arguably the most liberal country in Europe. Pedro Almodóvar was ideally placed to take advantage of the new morality and made films featuring gay, lesbian and transvestite characters, portrayed the Church and the police as corrupt, offered rape and murder as ingredients, and wove in the culture of film-making. *La Ley Del Deseo* (1987; *Law Of Desire*) was his breakthrough film in terms of international audiences, and the follow-up, *Mujere Al Borde De Un Ataque De Nervios* (1988; *Women On The Verge Of A Nervous Breakdown*) was an even bigger success.

Japanese cinema is partially made in a different way from western cinema – or at least it looks and feels very different from Classical Hollywood cinema since it doesn't fetishize continuity editing. At the same time the cinema is held to be very representative of the Japanese character – and a recurring theme is the fallout of the first atom bombs to be used in war. Most of the movies that have come from Japan have effectively been placed within the art cinema category, given that the aesthetics are thought to be so different; *Hiroshima, Mon Amour* (1959) offers a co-production with Alain Resnais of the French New Wave, and a meditation on the consequences for the individual of the Second World War. The same anxieties can be seen in the various Godzilla movies and arguably in *Akira* (1988), the breakthrough anime, and Shinya Tsukamoto's wonderful cyberpunk nightmare *Tetsuo* (1991). The four big names of Japanese cinema are Yasujiro Ozu (*Tokyo Monogatari, Tokyo Story*, 1952), Kenji Mizoguchi (*Saikaku Ichidai Onna, The Life Of Oharu*, 1952), Akira Kurosawa (*Shichinin No Samurai, Seven Samurai*, 1954) and

Nagisa Oshima (*Ai No Corrida, In The Realm Of The Senses*, 1976).

Australian Cinema

From three films to emerge from Australia in the early 1990s, you would gain a queer view of the country: *Strictly Ballroom* (1992), *Muriel's Wedding* (1994) and *The Adventures Of Priscilla, Queen Of The Desert* (1994) all contained elements of camp and featured to varying degrees fluid sexualities, a fixation with Abba, an ugly duckling narrative and a degree of post-modern pastiche and parody. These three quirky films, alongside the Oscar-winning *Shine* (1996), were all international box-office successes. But there is a darker strand to 1990s Australian cinema: the racism of skinhead culture in Footscray in *Romper Stomper* (1992, financed by New Zealand), the much darker exploration of sexuality, drugs and being of immigrant stock of *Head On* (1997), the paranoid, jump cut edited *Kiss or Kill* (1997) and the true-crime adaptation *Chopper* (2000). Taken together, we have a national cinema which is at the healthiest point in its history, perhaps even a victim of its own success. Australia is well placed to have a successful cinema – its English-language films can target its old colonial power, Britain, and the United States – but the commercial success of Australian cinema has waxed and waned over the century. The first feature film was made in Australia – *Story of the Kelly Gang* (1906) – and a reasonable number of films were shot in the middle of the silent era but production became increasingly sporadic after the Second World War.

The Overlanders (1946), *A Town like Alice* (1956) and *On the Beach* (1959) all had Australian settings but weren't locally financed. Serious production in Australia didn't get underway until the 1970s with a so-called New Wave, and the early films of Peter Weir, Fred Schepisi, Bruce Beresford and the two George Millers (confusingly).

This came about in part because of the establishment of the Australian Film Development Corporation (later the Australian Film Commission) in 1970 to finance the development of movies with government money; there were also funding bodies at the level of the individual state. This was supplemented by a series of tax rules which allowed investment to be written off, thus encouraging private funding of films. In the mid-1980s the tax rules changed, sending the industry into decline once more before the supplementing of the AFC with the Australian Film Finance Corporation in 1988. The AFFC has an annual grant to help finance films; other sources of revenue include various Australian television stations, most notably the Special Broadcasting Service (SBS), and production companies such as Southern Star. Many of the successful directors of the 1970s and early 1980s had been lured to America, for example Weir directing *Dead Poets Society* (1989) and *The Truman Show* (1998). In the mid-1980s only one film really broke through to international attention – *Crocodile Dundee* (1986) which took the eponymous hero from the Outback to New York and played with an Australian stereotype.

More recently, Australian cinema has been infiltrated by Hollywood studios, partially looking for more of the indie-style quirky films which have broken through to an international market since the start of the 1990s, but also to exploit local technicians in much the same way as British technicians were used on blockbuster films in the 1970s and 1980s. Fox (ultimately owned by Australian tycoon Rupert Murdoch) has studios in Sydney. Location for shooting *The Matrix* and its sequels also took place in Australian, perhaps an economically beneficial consequence of Warner Bros. teaming-up with Australian company Village Roadshow to finance the films. Meanwhile the films are distributed within Australia by Fox Columbia Tristar, Roadshow Film Distributors and United International Pictures, companies which have obvious links to American studios and distributors. The chains of cinemas include Hoyts, Village Roadshow (aka Warner Village and Greater Union) and Reading, another American-backed corporation. There is also a thriving art circuit in the major cities.

So what is the Australian national character as depicted in Australian films? The Australian is an immigrant or a descendent from an immigrant, predominately from waves of British colonisation over the last few centuries. Other European nationalities have moved to Australia, the Greek-Australian community being represented in *Death in Brunswick* (1990) and *Head On*, the latter also representing immigrants from Vietnam or Korea. There is perhaps the sense that western culture has been imposed on the landscape, that the cities are not quite real (see, again, *The Matrix*),

and the various road movies which should offer self-discovery for their heroes do not offer the same sense of transformation. Two of the drag queens in *Priscilla* simply learn from their exposure to the Outback and King's Canyon that there's no place like home, and the landscape is so alien that it seems not to be comprehended.

The films feature several of the national stereotypes of the Australian (male): the bushman (Crocodile Dundee), the pioneer, the ANZAC soldier (see *Gallipoli*, 1981), the larrikin or city-based delinquent (Ari in *Head On*) and the ocker – the resourceful, cheerful yet boorish and chauvinist working man, which shades into the battler. Two films directed by Robert Sitch, *The Castle* (1997) and *The Dish* (2001), developed with Working Dog, a team who had worked in television, show the battler at work. In the former the Kerrigan family face eviction from their idyllic home in order to allow an airport extension to be built. Dad Kerrigan reasons that this is his family's home, so it *can't* be demolished, and in the end he is successful, winning the (free) aid of a QC who is struck by Dad's common sense. The film can be criticised for its depiction of the Kerrigans – the ironic differences between the son's voice-over narration and what we see set the family up for ridicule. Further, the family's comparison of themselves to the dispossessed Aboriginals risks seeming racist – although in the extended family there are Greek- and Lebanese-descended characters. *The Dish* can seek comfort in nostalgia for a moment when Australia played a role on the world stage – the relaying of sounds and pictures back from the 1969 moon landing. When the radio telescope temporarily loses Apollo 11 shortly before an official visit from the American ambassador, the plucky members of the team imitate the astronaut and pretend nothing has gone wrong. It is the strait-laced NASA representative who is transformed during the course of the narrative and turns out to be a decent bloke after all, despite the framing narrative of Sam Neill (splendidly wearing a cardigan and smoking a pipe like a 50s dad) visiting the telescope as an old man. By then Working Dog had a three-movie, first-look deal with Village Roadshow, and rather knowingly used the American as the means of translating the film into a language which an international audience would be able to understand. The national character is laid bare for a world audience – to laugh at and admire.

Problems Discussing National Cinema

One of the problems of discussing national cinema is in defining what nation a particular film can be attributed to. The flow of international capital is only going to make this more and more complex, as non-American directors are funded by Hollywood and Hollywood follows tax shelters to new countries to film in, or searches for new technicians for the next generation of blockbusters.

The next problem is that for most of us our exposure to any nationality of cinema is going to be partial at best. Richard Lowenstein's adaptation of John Birmingham's flat-sharing memoirs *He Died with a Falafel in His Hand* (2000) set in Brisbane, Mel-

bourne and Sydney, was shown at an Italian film festival and was the closing film of the Melbourne Film Festival in 2001. A wider release has not yet occurred. It could be that only the most successful films will be imported, or in the case of art film, the artiest, so we don't see the whole spectrum from the most personal to the most commercial.

Finally there is the problem of identifying national characteristics. Production and distribution details are comparatively easy to locate, but the nature of the characteristic content of a film is harder to pin down. Edward Said, in his book *Orientalism* (1978), has identified a consistent set of values ascribed by the west to 'Orientals' – whether from Egypt or Arab countries, and by extension to Chinese, Japanese and other Far Eastern peoples. Even the terms Near, Middle and Far East are part of an Anglocentric bias that identifies the West as masculine, rational and modern and the east as feminine, irrational and old-fashioned. We risk imposing our own set of values and our own needs onto what we perceive in a nation. Equally, those within a particular culture may not best be placed to be objective about the specifics of their own national characteristics. It would be naïve to assume that a film straightforwardly represents a culture, or that an *auteur* is typical or definitive of a nation, but as more films are watched, so the detail can be filled in and inferred.

Andrew M. Butler

A version of this article appears as a chapter in the Pocket Essential Film Studies by Andrew M. Butler.

VISIONS OF THE APOCALYPSE

In his new book, Visions of the Apocalypse, *Wheeler Winston Dixon investigates America's attitude to the medium of film, in terms both of the country's predilection for spectacles of destruction and, as in this extract, the voracious appetite of the industry for economic gain at the expense of audience choice.*

Before the proliferation of electronic media made possible the distribution of films at minimal cost through DVD, cable, and the World Wide Web, world cinema and Hollywood cinema coexisted on a relatively equal basis. Each country's films had a different theatrical distribution system within the United States, depending on language, point of origin, and the perceived artistic merit of the film in question. British films, such as *The Loneliness of the Long Distance Runner* (1962), *The Knack* (1965), *Carry On Nurse* (1958), *Tom Jones* (1963), and others required no subtitles and generally were accorded a wide release. French films usually appeared in major metropolitan centers with subtitles and in outlying districts with a dubbed version. Italian films such as *Open City* (1945; original title *Roma, città aperta*, 1945), *La*

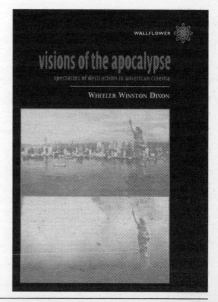

Dolce Vita (1960), *Juliet of the Spirits* (1965; original title *Giulietta degli spiriti*, 1965), *Big Deal on Madonna Street* (1958; original title *I soliti ignoti*, 1958), *8 1/2* (1963), and other films designated "instant classics" by US critics were generally subtitled, whereas titles such as *The Day the Sky Exploded* (1961; *La Morte viene dallo spazio*, 1958), *Black Sunday* (1961; original title *La maschera del demonio*, 1960), *Hercules in the Haunted World* (1964; original title *Ercole al centro della terra*, 1961), *My Son, the Hero* (1963; original title *Arrivano i titani*, 1961), and other more commercial fare were routinely dubbed. This general pattern of "quality" versus "commercial appeal" governed the linguistic fate of most non-US films. When *Yojimbo the Bodyguard* (1962; original title *Yojimbo*, 1961), *High and Low* (1963, original title *Tengoku to jigoku*, 1963), *Woman in the Dunes* (1964; original title *Suna no onna*, 1964), *Kwaidan* (1964; original title *Kaidan*, 1964), and other "quality" Japanese films appeared in the United States, they were subtitled; the *Godzilla* films, on the other hand, suffered from atrocious dubbing, usually done by the Titra Sound Studios in New York, which specialized in dubbing foreign imports.

Indian films remained, for the most part, within the boundaries of their own nation, except for the films of Satyajit Ray, which were always subtitled; Ingmar Bergman, for many years the sole representative in the United States of Swedish cinema, was also scrupulously titled. German films generally were subtitled, unless they were cheap programmers in the long-running Edgar Wallace mystery series, in which case they were dubbed. The same fate befell Hong Kong action films in the 1970s; an extremely slipshod, often asynchronous dubbing job ensured that films would reach only grind house audiences. The dubbing or subtitling of a film often determined its critical fate, as well as its commercial destiny. Dubbed films were almost universally excoriated by the critics and thus by the audiences who read their reviews; subtitled films, on the other hand, were usually afforded a modicum of respect. International co-productions were guaranteed an even warmer reception at the US box office, particularly if they featured an American star. Hammer Films used this strategy in its early British films of the 1950s, casting Tom Conway, Brian Donlevy, Alex Nicol, Hillary Brooke, and other fading stars to ensure US release. Occasionally, a film made outside the United States would be afforded a measure of commercial viability through its choice of director, as in the case of British director Thorold Dickinson's *Hill 24 Doesn't Answer* (1955; original title *Giv'a 24 Eina Ona*, 1955), which dealt with the turmoil surrounding the early days on the state of Israel. *Hill 24 Doesn't Answer* received solid distribution in both the United States and Great Britain, but hedged its bets by being shot in English (using British star Edward Mulhare as one of the leads), although the film was officially classified as an Israeli production.

Thus, even through the early 1970s, when Roger Corman's New World Pictures functioned as one of the last surviving conduits of foreign theatrical distribution in the United States, most famously co-producing and distributing Ingmar Bergman's *Cries and Whispers* (1972; original title *Viskningar och rop*, 1972) when no other US distributor would touch it, non-US films had a chance to crack the US market, albeit an increasingly slim one as the decades rolled on. With the introduction of pay television, however, in the mid to late 1970s, theatrical distribution was no longer a financial necessity, and the number of "art" houses in the United States began to dwindle. In the first part of the 21st century, they have almost completely vanished—not only in the United States, but in Europe and Asia as well. At the same time, the number of repertory theatres also declined. Audiences could no longer see the classics of the past in their original 35mm format.

I remember the first time I saw Charles Crichton's *The Lavender Hill Mob* (1951) in a revival house in 1961 on a double bill with Robert Dhéry's just-released *The American Beauty* (1961; *La belle Américaine*, 1961), allowing me to see both films on equal terms—the then-current and the classic projected in their proper formats. The experience, of course, was overwhelming and nothing at all like the off-the-cuff, "background noise" effect of viewing a film on DVD on a television, no matter how gargantuan the screen. A very real argument can be made

that all films that originated in 35mm should be screened in that format alone if one wants to approximate anything like the original viewing experience available to audiences when the film was first produced.

As another example of this phenomenon, in early 2002 I travelled to Los Angeles for a series of screenings at the American Cinematheque, coordinated by Dennis Bartok. On the bill that week were screenings of Val Guest's *The Day the Earth Caught Fire*, with its original colour prologue and epilogue intact, and Mario Bava's *Planet of the Vampires* (1965; original title *Terrore nello spazio*, 1965), the latter presented in a brand new 35mm print. Both films are readily available on video and shown constantly on television; *The Day the Earth Caught Fire*, which is in CinemaScope, has even been screened on commercial television in letterbox format. Both films sit on my shelves in DVD format, but nothing prepared me for the shock of seeing them projected again, for the first time in nearly 40 years, on a large screen with first-rate International Alliance of Theatrical Stage Employees (IATSE) union projectionists in front of an appreciative audience. Rather than viewing the films as a solitary spectator, I was allowed to experience them as part of an audience, as a social and communal act.

Subtle touches that would have drifted past my eyes on the small screen—a sudden optical effect, a striking composition, a deftly edited dialogue sequence—appeared anew to my eyes, seen in the proper size and format again. These films were never meant to be seen on the small screen; they were spatially and emotionally designed for a heroic canvas. Thus, as the director Roy Ward Baker has commented, although you can "inspect" a film in DVD/televisual format, you cannot really judge its effectiveness or participate in it on an emotional or artistic level of any real consequence. The DVDs we buy are mere *aides de memoire* of experiences we once shared with others and now are unable to authentically recall. In an interview with this author in 1994, Baker discussed his own film, *A Night to Remember* (1958), perhaps the best of the *Titanic* films. Having just seen the film in a retrospective of his work, Baker noted that

> I had seen *A Night to Remember*, obviously, several times on television since I made it, but I made it, after all, in 1958. And since that time, I'd never seen it on a big screen... And the effect of seeing it again on the big screen, after all this time, it shows you the whole difference between movies and television... You see, when you see a film on television on a small screen, you're not in the film at all. You inspect it. You can look at it. You can enjoy it to a certain extent, but you'll never be involved in it. You can judge it; you can say, "Well, that was a good movie." But it's an entirely objective judgment; it's not subjective because you're not being subjected to the film.

It's almost like viewing a photocopy of a Caravaggio painting; no copy can ever do the original justice. What makes this all the more frustrating is that economics, not artistic forces, is driving the current digitization of the cinema, even as studio heads and archivists pay token homage to cinema's past. Thus, when one speaks of a particular film being "available" on DVD or another home video format, one should more correctly say that an inferior copy of the original is available for viewing, rather than the film itself. An even more insidious factor is that although the American Film Institute and other organizations celebrate the heritage of the moving image, contemporary Hollywood studios are busily strip-mining the past to create "new" product. In doing so, many production entities consciously engage in legal maneuvering to keep the source film off the market, even in 16mm and 35mm formats, in the ostensible hope that newer audiences, unaware of the original film, will be unaware of its existence. An example of this is the remake of Norman Jewison's *Rollerball* (1975; remake 2002). Although the first film was deeply flawed, its vision of a future world without war, dominated by violent recreational sport, carried a direct political message to the audience. The remake, which centers only on the game of Rollerball itself as an extreme sport, eschews the theme of global corporate domination entirely. Does one really need to ask why?

At the same time, a great deal of evidence exists that contemporary audiences recognize the recycled quality of the current cinema—and reject it. They would go to see something else if they had the choice, but they do not. As Rick Lyman noted in an article in the *New York Times* in 2001:

> Something profound is happening at the megaplexes, and it has little to do with what appears on the screen. Rather, it is about how those movies are being seen.
>
> The summer hits of 2001 are making about as much money as hits from previous summers, but they are making it quicker, making more of it than ever on opening weekend. Movies are opening on more screens, generating staggering grosses and then plummeting off the radar. Many executives in Hollywood see this trend, which they call "front loading," as a fundamental change in the way summer movies are being watched... In the future, when digital distribution comes and movies are shipped electronically rather than on metal reels, these trends will only be magnified, as they will when studios become more adept at opening films not merely all over the country but all over the world on the same day.

Lyman goes on to demonstrate how newer films open in 3,000 theatres simultaneously to avoid Internet piracy and gain as much audience penetration as possible before negative word of mouth sets in. This strategy, originally created by James Nicholson and Samuel Z. Arkoff of American International Pictures (AIP) in the mid-to-late 1950s, was originally dubbed "saturation booking." Nicholson and Arkoff had no illusions about AIP's product; they knew that what they were selling was commercial junk and that only a hit-and-run booking pattern would reap maximum return on their investment. Whereas major studios in the 1950s often "platformed" their films, opening them in major cities in "road show" engagements at higher ticket prices before releasing them throughout the United States and subsequently foreign territories, AIP's smash-and-grab tactics gave the company a solid cash flow to produce new product, essential in what was a very thinly capitalized operation. Such AIP films as *I Was a Teenage Werewolf* (1957), *I Was a Teenage Frankenstein* (1957), and *Ghost of Dragstrip Hollow* (1959) have become exploitation classics, films that accurately pegged audience expectations and delivered what the majors at the time refused to do: adolescent entertainment. Made on six-day schedules and budgets in the $100,000 range, AIP's films constituted a genuine threat to the majors, which had just been deprived of their guaranteed theatrical outlets with the advent of the consent decree of 1948. AIP offered exhibitors advantageous terms, immediate delivery, and splashy ad campaigns designed to appeal to the widest possible audience.

By the 1970s, when AIP was absorbed into Filmways, the majors had caught onto AIP's strategy and began aggressively duplicating it. In 1975, *Jaws* opened in 409 theaters in the United States and did spectacular business. The budget was higher, the advertising costs greater, the number of prints more than AIP could ever have afforded. In 1983, *Star Wars: Episode VI—Return of the Jedi* opened in 1,002 locations. In 1996, *Mission: Impossible* opened in 3,000 theatres; in 2000, *Mission: Impossible II* opened in more than 3,500 theatres. *The Mummy Returns* (2001) started in 3,401 theatres; *Shrek* (2001) in 3,587 theatres; and *Rush Hour 2* in 3,118 theatres. By the summer of 2002, *Spider-Man* was able to open in 3,615 theatres simultaneously on as many as 7,500 multiplex screens. In the film's first three days, it grossed $114 million. But how long it can hold on to that kind of audience is a real question. *Planet of the Apes* (2001) opened to $68.5 million, but fell by 60% in its second week at the box office. *The Mummy Returns* fell 50% in its second week; *Pearl Harbor* (2001) fell 50% in its second week; *Lara Croft: Tomb Raider* (2001) fell 59% in its second week. People rush to the theatre on the week a film opens, but then just as rapidly desert it when the next blockbuster comes along. Studios are delighted with this phenomenon because opening weekend contracts typically stipulate a 90/10 split of the profits, with 90% of the first week's profits going directly to the production entity. The theatre makes its money on the concession stand, as it always has, and by the second week, an 80/20 split, again favouring the studio, usually kicks in. But by this time, another film comes roaring out of the gate, and the game starts all over again, week after exhausting week. Internet piracy only adds to the urgency in getting a film out to as many paying customers as quickly as possible; in the three days before the opening of *Planet of the Apes,* a complete version of the film, pirated from a stolen 35mm print, was circulating on the Web. AIP in the 1950s and 1960s would play their films territory by territory across the United States until every last dime had been extracted from the audience. The majors in the 1970s and 1980s could afford far larger "breaks," increasing the chances that regardless how bad the reviews were, the film would be a hit. In the days before the Internet, the studios could also follow the seasons around the globe, opening a summer film in Australia in December, typically the warmest time of the year down under. No more. With piracy, the ubiquity of the Web, and the complete interconnectivity of contemporary audience and fan base, a film must open everywhere, all over the world, simultaneously.

From *Visions of the Apocalypse* by Wheeler Winston Dixon, published in September 2003 by Wallflower Press (£12.99).

FILM SCORE FOCUS

O f all the 'Technical' Academy Awards, the Best Score Category has created most controversy over the years. Part of the problem has been the contention that it's the only category studios can use to re-sell their product. The addition of an 'Oscar Winner' label to an album's marketing has enormous cashback potential. Yet before a score has even won, it's all down to the marketing. Legend tells how Michael Nyman lost out being nominated for *The Piano* (1993) because of an overly aggressive campaign although all the evidence points to a similarly bullish campaign on behalf of *The Full Monty* in 1997 – the eventual winner).

It's because of such goings-on that the category has sometimes been split into two or three separate sections. This often followed a string of years when someone in the Academy hierarchy disapproved of

a trend toward financially-motivated popularity. In the mid Nineties, a constant series of wins by Alan Menken for his Disney scores in the Best Original Score category (*The Little Mermaid*, 1989, *Beauty and the Beast*, 1991, *Aladdin*, 1992, *Pocahantas*, 1995) was responded to by splitting it into Dramatic Score and Musical or Comedy Score. Ironically, this was done just as Menken had readied himself to move on and the period of critical favour for Disney was waning.

2003 nearly faced a last minute category crisis. Voters were confused by being told in advance that sequel scores should no longer be eligible, the thinking being that repetition of previously written thematic material should not warrant being rewarded as 'original'. While *Lord of the Rings* composer Howard Shore rapidly pieced together a legal reaction to this nonsense, and the motion was quietly retracted before anyone went to vote, the damage had been done. *The Two Towers* didn't get its nomination, despite Shore having actually won the year before for *The Fellowship of the Ring*.

Several other Awards have so far managed to stay ahead of the Oscars. This year The Golden Globes favoured the scores for *Far From Heaven, Frida, The Hours, Rabbit Proof Fence* and *The 25th Hour*. All were met with approval, but the absence of *The Two Towers* did not go unnoticed. The BAFTA nominations however, raised many eyebrows: *Catch Me if You Can, Chicago* (featuring numerous previously existing songs), *Gangs of New York* (a collection of material from multiple sources), *The Hours* and *The Pianist* (composer Wojciech Kilar's score is secondary to far more use of Chopin) all competed in the Best Original Score category.

So when the Oscar nominations were announced, the movie music community was somewhat prepared for an element of controversy. With only one exception however, the five nominees were pleasingly deserving. It was as if a fight long spoiled for had simply fizzled out. Sure enough *The Two Towers* was missing, but there had been enough warning to expect as much. The real sigh of relief was that Shore's participation in *Gangs of New York* wasn't being offered in its stead, since that piece was actually written before Scorcese's picture ever existed and was part of a rag bag of musical ideas drafted in to replace a rejected Elmer Bernstein score.

The five nominees were:

Frida - Elliot Goldenthal
Catch Me If You Can - John Williams
Far From Heaven - Elmer Bernstein
The Hours - Philip Glass
The Road To Perdition - Thomas Newman

The exception I mentioned was *The Hours*, which is the only one to have appeared in all three Award groups mentioned above. For his score, Glass incorporated some of his previously existing work, as acknowledged in the film's credits. Naturally, reaction tended toward thinking it therefore had no real chance of winning. After the 'no sequels' argument, surely this should have fall down on the same criteria (i.e. not being entirely 'original')? This was only a small offence in the grand scheme of things, and was neatly balanced by the remaining four nominees.

All were deemed nicely worthy, but without pause, anyone asked would state Elmer Bernstein was a certainty, mainly because out of his thirteen previous nominations, the 80 year old statesman of the craft only ever won in 1969 for *Thoroughly Modern Millie*. Weighted next was the trusty John Williams / Steven Spielberg factor, which had mined Oscar gold many times before. Incredibly, this actually represented Williams' 41st nomination, out of which he's won 5 times. Odds were understandably stacked in support of the possibility. Then came relative newcomer Thomas Newman, who after unsuccessfully competing against himself in 1995 with *The Shawshank Redemption* and *Little Women*, followed the next year with *Unstrung Heroes* and *American Beauty* soon after. It seemed like he was in with a shot at least.

All of which left Elliot Goldenthal's *Frida* pretty much at the tail end of most observers' expectations. Especially since the composer's song from the movie ("Burn it Blue") was a reasonable contender in the Best Original Song category. Thus when Goldenthal's name was called out, it was frankly stunning. I admire the man's work very much and in the years he'd been nominated for *Interview With the Vampire* (1994) and *Michael Collins* (1996) he would have been a worthy winner. Then in his acceptance speech, I wondered if there had been more at work around *Frida* than I'd appreciated. 'For you, Mexico!' he cried from the podium. In an Oscar round-up, one Hollywood journalist explained with insider perspective: 'I hadn't heard one word from anyone that he was favoured. Someone said that he'd worked the Academy

circuit heavily and basically politicked his ass off. This isn't to put down his work — it was just a total surprise to hear his name called out.'

So in what way will controversy surround the 2004 Awards? Actually, I can already see it coming. Any further political manoeuvring around the category will likely have more closely observed results anyway. The big issue is that for external reasons, the Awards have been moved forward to February 29th. This means that the Music category submissions deadline is now December 1st. Since *The Return of the King* doesn't even open until December 17th, Howard Shore looks likely to be disappointed again and a lot of film music admirers will be wishing this category would just settle down without interference.

Paul Tonks

KAMERA

www.**kamera.co.uk**, the self-styled 'intelligent film web site', goes offline with the first issue of its new bi-monthly magazine incarnation. Each issue leads with a 'themed' section and also includes an extensive article on a major film-maker, regular columns on film festivals, documentary and short film, and a comprehensive reviews section featuring all the latest books and DVDs, making **kamera** the essential companion to world cinema today.